Gardening for Abundance

Gardening for Abundance

Your Guide to Cultivating a
Bountiful Veggie Garden and a Happier Life

Brian Brigantti
Founder of Redleaf Ranch

PAGE STREET
PUBLISHING CO.

PAGE STREET
PUBLISHING CO.

First published in 2024 by
Page Street Publishing Co.
27 Congress Street, Suite 1511
Salem, MA 01970
www.pagestreetpublishing.com

Distributed by Macmillan, sales in Canada by The Canadian Manda Group.

28   27   26   25   24   1   2   3   4   5

ISBN-13: 978-1-64567-953-0
ISBN-10: 1-64567-953-5

Library of Congress Control Number: 2023936580

Cover and book design by Vienna Mercedes Gambol for Page Street Publishing Co.
Photography and illustrations by Brian Brigantti

Printed and bound in USA

To my mother; my younger brother;
and my partner, Domonick—my greatest supporters
and inspiration.

Contents

Preface

So many years of my life were spent searching for my purpose, when all I had to do was look down. All I had to do was scratch into the Earth and feel her coolness between my fingers. If I could go back in time and speak to my younger self, I'd tell him to remember. Remember the joy you felt turning rocks to see what hidden wonders were waiting for you. Remember the peace you felt walking through the lone forest on the outskirts of the city. Remember the songs of cardinals that echoed through our upbringing, bringing us solace in all the chaos. *Ree-ree-tu-tu-tu-tu.*

I'll never forget breaking ground for the first time. The pandemic had sparked a need to grow our own food on our newly acquired land, far away from the confines of the big city. I had never gardened a day in my life, but now was the time to learn. Without much thought, spades pierced the Earth, revealing the warm-colored ground below. I picked up the red clay in my hand and felt it crumble between my fingers. I caught a light aroma of the soil and jolted. A vision of me as a child raced to the front of my mind: playing in the dirt looking for bugs as the sweet scent of the Earth filled my nose. I snapped back to reality with tears in my eyes. I remembered. This is where I was always meant to be. The Earth had called me home.

It's been four years since that moment, and life has never been the same. My days now revolve around working the land and cultivating her abundance. I can no longer imagine a life without a garden growing in it. Living on this very special piece of land has shown me firsthand how much abundance it can provide if we choose to care for it. The seed of responsibility has been planted within me and I've been entrusted as a steward of this land. I am no master gardener, but I care deeply for Mother Earth and she has rewarded me with the gift of her abundance. I have bled, sweat and wept working this land. Through it all, I have learned so many valuable lessons about Mother and how we can coexist in harmony. The goal of this book is to share the experiences in the garden that have shaped who I am today, gardening techniques and the wisdom the Earth has whispered in my ear.

I hope that reading these words inspires you to live a life in tune with the abundance that exists all around us. *Allow me to show you how to live a life of abundance.*

9

Chapter 1

Creating a Life of Abundance

Before diving into the world of gardening, it's imperative that I share the ways of creating abundance in all aspects of your life. Having a mindset of abundance allows the overflow of prosperity, love and light to pour into our lives. Having a firm understanding and grasp of these knowings will allow you to navigate through your gardens and life with more ease and grace.

Tuning in to the Abundance

Abundance! Those three syllables somehow manage to perfectly encapsulate an overwhelming feeling of prosperity and gratitude. It's magnetic and transcends far beyond the reaches of our gardens. Every time the word leaves my lips, I can't help but smile. But one may ask, "What does abundance mean?" Simply put: Abundance is having everything you could possibly ever need and more. It's never having to worry that there isn't or won't be enough. Think of it as an overflow, breaching the edges of desire and pouring over. Everything that we could ever possibly need is here, on this Earth; all we need to do is reach for it and claim it. Working with the land has shown me just how generous Mother Nature can be, providing all our sustenance. Better yet, she wraps it all into perfectly sized juicy orbs. A gift, ready to be enjoyed.

But you see, having abundance is so much more than whatever we can feel within our grasp. If we tune ourselves to the *frequency of abundance*, we align ourselves with the limitless potential this marvelous world has to offer. Abundance is so much more than what we hold in our hands after a hard day's work or a successful harvest. Abundance is a state of mind. A state of *being*.

By design, we are abundant beings. We have the power to think, connect, cultivate, speak and create. Anything and everything that we could ever desire is possible. All we have to do is *believe it*. Unfortunately, the belief that we have it all has been shrouded by the capitalist ideology that has plagued our consciousness. In this consumerist world, we are told we always need more. We're constantly beckoned by the thought that what we have is never enough. Everywhere we look, we're told satisfaction comes from material things: the shiny new smartphone, the trendy new beauty product, the latest designer collection, the fancy new car. From the day we enter this world, we are conditioned to focus on what is lacking in our lives and believe that true satisfaction must be bought. It's a tedious cycle of consumption and dissatisfaction. Society has become so attuned to consumption, we've completely lost touch with the abundance that already exists all around us. Rather than being taught to be grateful for what we do have, we are constantly reminded of what we are *lacking*. To live a life of abundance is to be grateful for where we are in our lives now and everything that has led to this moment. To live a life of abundance is to understand that life is *already abundant*. To live a life of abundance is to visualize the life of our dreams and know that it's already ours.

Because modern society runs on consumerism, it can be especially challenging to recalibrate our mindset to one of abundance. An attunement to a life of *lack* chips away at our confidence, motivation and creativity. Our lust for life dwindles away when we constantly believe that what we have is never enough. Our dreams for a better life drift further and further away when we believe the path there is out of reach, locked away behind the doors of materialistic ideologies. I used to lead a life of lack, never feeling I could reach my ultimate goals of success, not realizing that that idea of success was not even my own, but one fed to me by a capitalist society. Then, one fateful day, the teachings of Abraham Hicks echoed through my ears: *"What you believe becomes your reality."*

Those words shook me to my core. They planted a seed within me. I had been so focused on the *destination* that I completely forgot the importance of the *journey*. If the beliefs in my everyday life weren't truly aligned with what I was striving for, how could I ever conceive of getting there? Rather than focusing on the abundance that lay ahead, I had to shift my focus to the abundance around me *now*. Rather than feeling that what I had wasn't enough, I started expressing my gratitude for it all. *I'm grateful for my morning cup of coffee, I'm grateful I have shoes to wear, I'm grateful I have a job that can pay for the life I'm living, I'm grateful for my friends, I'm grateful for my family, I'm grateful for the air I breathe, I'm grateful for the water I drink, I'm grateful for the shirt on my back, I'm grateful I can walk, I'm grateful for the sun beaming down.* Every time a lacking thought came my way, I countered it with a thought of abundance, with gratitude. *I am satisfied with where my life is now. Every day is a gift.*

The fuller I believed my life was, the fuller it became. I began believing in the abundance all around me and it began to attract more abundance into my life. No matter what life threw my way, I firmly believed and still believe that it's all part of the plan. Life flows and we must follow.

Now that I found myself in the stream of gratitude, the next thing I focused on was my own definition of success. When I closed my eyes and envisioned the finish line, what did I see? We are the creators of our own reality. The only thing I cared about when I closed my eyes was that what I saw at the peak was a dream that was purely my own. A destination purely aligned with who I am and what makes me happy. No matter what I do in this life, the light guiding my actions is to positively impact the lives that I reach. Life should be joyful, truthful, loving and abundant. That is what I believe, so it is.

Whatever your dream may be, the ultimate goal is to make sure it is *yours*. Having a firm grounding in my belief and what I wanted while also being grateful for the abundance already in my life allowed some really unique doors to fade into my path. The door that was knocking the loudest was the one calling me home, back to Mother Nature. My entire life has been spent in the concrete veins of a city; it was time for a change. It was time to remember my roots. The shift from city life to country life was scary, but I wasn't about to let fear stop me from pursuing my dreams. I knew I was on the right path. How did I know? *It felt good.*

A harvest full of abundance.

Looking back, I am so grateful that I listened to Mother Nature's call. At the time, I was deeply tuned in to the frequency of abundance and Mother was ready to show me just how abundant life can be. Working in the garden has deeply affirmed the mind-set of abundance. Mother Nature is the pure embodiment of abundance itself. Everything we will ever need, she provides. The purest way to tap into that stream of abundance is by expressing our gratitude to her for all she gives us. Expressing that gratitude is an act of defiance in a world designed to make us feel ungrateful. I can't help but feel wealthy when I let Mother know just how much I appreciate all that she has given me. When I'm tending to the garden, I envision the abundance before planting the first seed. I nourish the soil, my token of gratitude to the Earth for all that she has given and will continue to give. When we recognize and express gratitude for that abundance, we allow more of it to channel into our lives. *Abundance creates abundance.*

The Power of Alignment

To truly tap into the power of abundance, we must have a deep understanding of ourselves. To have a deep understanding of self, it's important that we take the time to step back and reflect on the experiences we have lived through. When we make the decision to transcend to Earth and live this life, we already know what we've come here to do. Ultimately, the purpose of life is to experience every possible moment we can because through our experiences is where we learn the most about ourselves. And I don't just mean the good experiences, I mean all of it. The good, the bad and the ugly. They all help shape who we become in this life.

The real test is being able to look deep within ourselves and decide how we will allow these experiences to influence us. The way I see it, there are two paths we can follow that guide us to our final destination. I use the term *final destination* loosely because, do we truly ever get there? What I mean is, what will be light at the end of the tunnel—your light or someone else's? To manifest the abundance destined for your life, you have to really know yourself. You have to know what you *desire* the most. Only then can you truly see all that

is meant for you. It can be easy to be swept up in the current of someone else's dreams and desires for your life, but there will come a point in your life when you'll have to decide whether the desires of others align with your own. I believe that all of us are born with a strong internal guidance system. A guidance system that is led by our spirit. Call it that little voice in your head that is always telling you what's the right thing to do. The more you listen to that voice, the stronger it gets.

Sometimes, it can be confusing to understand that what is "right" or "best" for you doesn't necessarily mean it's going to be the easiest path to choose. It can be a path of sacrifice, challenges, adversity or even rebellion. But the greatest thing you can do for yourself is to listen to that little voice that is guiding you, fighting for you, waiting for you to choose you. That doesn't mean it'll be easy. In fact, it can even be terrifying, but on the other side of fear is abundance. It can be hard choosing yourself because it means you have to leave certain people or situations behind, especially if it's those that you love. Think of yourself as a little seedling in a tiny pot. You can grow comfortably there for a while, but eventually your roots will begin to grow larger and need more room to grow. The pot must be shed and you must plant yourself in a place with more room to grow. Then, once you've become the beautiful tree you were meant to be, you can share your fruit with others. You see, we have to make those difficult decisions to learn who we are and what we desire most. That desire for a life that is written by you will propel you forward.

The reason I bring all of this up is that, when I finally got to experience the peace and quiet of my first garden, when I surrendered to that peace, a lot of unexpected feelings surfaced. For what seemed like the first time in my life, I finally got the chance to stop. In that stillness I realized that I finally had the opportunity to feel safe. To let my guard down and just *be*. I had been in fight-or-flight mode for as long as I could remember, but in my garden, that didn't matter anymore. Nothing else mattered, actually. I was at ease and present in that moment. It was nice while it lasted. But before long, a strange feeling of guilt started fluttering through me. A guilt that I had been carrying for a long time, and it wasn't even mine. I had worked so hard to get to this very place and I knew I was worthy of it, but the conditionings of society that have been chiseled into my mind were not allowing me to enjoy this place. *I couldn't sit still; a part of me felt that I had to keep working.* That's when I realized just how much I had been conditioned to believe in a way of life that wasn't my own. I thought, *I deserve to just be. I deserve to enjoy this moment. I deserve everything good that comes to my life.* I snapped myself out of that guilt and cherished that moment of clarity, but that was the start of a long road ahead of unlearning the ways of a life that weren't mine. Long ago, I made the decision to let my spirit lead, but through the chaos of the journey, I never had a moment to stop and appreciate where it had led me. Until now. I knew then that I had to prioritize the time to be present and face whatever came with it.

It is powerful to be present with yourself. It's not easy to face parts of ourselves that we're ashamed of or beliefs that no longer serve us, beliefs that were never our own to begin with yet somehow have become deeply etched into us. To face those harsh truths, to unlearn them and to actively decide how you want to live, is no easy feat. You have to learn to trust yourself. The more you choose the things that feel good to you, the things that align with you, the easier it will become to determine what those things are. The steps we take back to our true self get us closer and closer to understanding what we truly desire in this life. The closer we get to feeling that deep desire, the closer we get to tapping into that frequency of abundance. Abundance manifests itself the more aligned we are to our desires, and the only way to know what you desire is to know yourself.

In the chaos that permeates the world, it can be challenging to find moments of stillness that allow us to truly be with ourselves. That is why it is so important that we prioritize making the time to reach that stillness and become present with self. Here are a few practices I use to align to my higher self:

- *Meditation:* In the morning, before I pick up my phone and let the noise of the world into my mind, I sit up, take in a deep breath and bask in the stillness. I focus on my breathing, listening to the air pass through my nostrils and feeling it leave my body as I exhale. Sometimes, I feel parts of my body and breathe into those places that need to be loved: My heart, my belly, my head. Sometimes, if I can't seem to get into the flow of my breath, I focus on something around me, maybe the songs of birds outside my window or the air conditioner gently blowing into the room. The goal is to calm the mind and be still. Reclaim your power every morning by stepping into your higher divine self so you can take on the day in alignment.

- *Hand Watering My Garden:* There are many tasks in the garden, but my favorite is hand watering the plants. There's something so fulfilling about being the hand that nurtures my children. It's nurturing to nurture. But the reason I love it so much is that, for a few hours a day, I can be fully present in the world around me as I tend to each individual plant. In that peace, I'm able to release any feelings that are weighing on me as I bask in the gratitude of the abundance all around.

- *Be in Nature:* I understand not everyone has access to a garden, but connecting with the natural world is essential. Our soul needs it. For days when I feel overwhelmed with the amount of work that needs to get done or the unsteadiness of the world, I disconnect from it all and go for a hike deep into the mountains. There's something so freeing about walking through the forest and knowing I don't have service on my phone. My tether to the world severed, finally alone. As I reach the peak and see the ocean of green cascading below, I take a deep breath of gratitude. Finally, with no one to judge me and no phone to distract me, I can just be.

- *Create:* The greatest form of release for my thoughts, my worries and my emotions has always been through my art. Whatever words cannot express, my artwork can. As humans, we have the innate ability to create; we are all meant to. Our creativity is literally our soul expressed. When we relinquish the worry of being critiqued and just allow ourselves to be fully present in the moment of creation, we get so much closer to self. And what is so beautiful about our creativity is that there are countless ways to express it. Pick up a paintbrush, bust a move, belt a hymn, start a garden, write about a magical world, paint your face, wear that sequined top, CREATE! Relinquish all fears and set your spirit free.

These are but a few practices that ground me and help me realign with myself. It's imperative that we take the time to process emotions, experience new things, and most importantly, do the things that bring us joy. The moment you decide to live for yourself and do the things that make you happy is the moment abundance begins to pour into your life. While it's important to serve our communities and help others, there has to be time we dedicate to ourselves. We have to fill up our glass so we can pour the abundance that has been poured into us. To tune into that frequency, we must be present with ourselves and remember who we really are. The frequency of our true higher selves and that of abundance are one and the same, for we are abundant beings. *All we have to do is remember.*

Overcoming Failure

The date is March 24, 2020. Clouds blanket the sky as I arrive at what is starting to look like a garden. Four beds are in the ground and the form of others are etched into the Earth. In my hands, I have a tray of 10 Tuscan kale plants that I am itching to plant. I am overtaken by the rush of excitement and I immediately begin to plant all my kale, completely disregarding whatever their labels say they need. My trowel begins piercing the soil, making way for the kale. I release a kale plantling from its pot and the root ball fills the palm of my hand. Without even thinking, I place my kale in the hole and bury it in. Not even a hand's length apart, I pierce the soil again and make way for the next kale plantling. And again, I dig, I plant, I dig, I plant, I dig, I plant, I dig and I plant.

With a single drop of sweat dripping down my temple, I stand and look at my proud achievement. A beautiful cluster of tightly packed kale. All their leaves touching as if holding hands and welcoming one another to their new home. *How sweet*, I think. I move along to work on the new beds taking shape and continue with my day.

A week passes. I come back to check on my kale and there hasn't been much progress. I think, *Maybe they just need time to settle*, and leave it at that. I check back on the kale the following week, and still no progress. One more week passes and still very little to no growth. At this point, I know something is wrong. How can three weeks have passed and my kale has not even budged?

I take my concerns to Google and look up what kale plants need to grow their best, because in my excitement, I threw away their labels. The first thing I see on my screen: "Kale plants need at least 18 inches (45 cm) of spacing in between them." Dumbfounded, I look up back to my kale and laugh at how tightly bunched together they all are. *Oh.*

I grab my trowel and a tape measure, and I get to work. One by one, I uproot every individual kale plant and lay them out exactly 18 inches apart. Once I was sure that my spacing was right, I dug them all back in one by one. That day, I learned about the importance of spacing: If your plants are too close together, they will inevitably compete for water, nutrients and sunlight. That simple mistake of planting them too close could have really discouraged me from planting anything else, but I took the opportunity to do a little more research and try again.

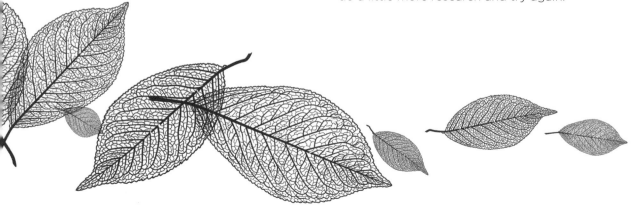

Sadly, during the replanting, I shook up the roots a little too much on some of my kale plants and they didn't survive. Looking at those sad wilted plants, I was filled with disappointment, completely disregarding the plants that had settled in and were starting to grow. I was so focused on my failure that I didn't even notice my success. My partner, Dom, came up to me and asked why I was so down. I explained to him that a few of my kale plants died, and he giggled. He said, "Well, throw them in the compost! They'll break down and you'll be able to use them in the garden again. That's the beautiful thing about nature: Nothing goes to waste. When one thing dies, it simply breaks down so that it can bring life once again."

That simple truth about Nature snapped me out of my state of disappointment. He was completely right! And what's more, it was a pure reflection of how we should view and overcome our own failures. The garden taught me that even within our failures, there is potential to grow. We cannot allow the fear of failure to hold us back from experiencing the abundance that waits on the other side. Yes, things may not necessarily go our way or however we planned it, but the end result can still be full of abundance. Since my kale fiasco, I have killed dozens upon dozens more plants and I have made many mistakes, but rather than dwelling in the disappointment of those failures, I simply threw those plants in the compost and tried again! This time, with newfound wisdom that I didn't have before those experiences.

When it comes to gardening and, really, anything in life, *we cannot be afraid to fail.* Failure can actually be what propels us into a level of success that we wouldn't have been able to experience if things just went our way. At the end of the day, we have to experience failure. We have to make mistakes because, without them, we wouldn't be nearly as appreciative of our achievements when we finally reach them. We are stronger, we are wiser and we are better when we give ourselves the grace to make mistakes and learn from them. If things don't go as planned, just throw it in the compost and try again.

Balance: The Exchange of Energy

A thriving ecosystem is a balanced ecosystem. When we turn to the natural world, she shows us that within a thriving forest there is a delicate balance between creatures, plants and the life within the soil. Every organism has a role to play, and within those roles, there is a balance between what they give and what they take. If a certain organism begins to take too much, it can throw off the scales of reciprocity in the forest. At the top of the food chain, we may find a hawk or a bobcat whose role is to satiate its hunger by hunting a variety of prey, such as deer, rabbits or squirrels. The prey that these predators hunt can be voracious eaters, endlessly grazing on the foliage that fills the forest. If these predators were to disappear, these foliage feeders could quickly decimate an area. Now, other organisms that depended on those plants have to struggle to survive. And, vice versa, if the predators overhunted, there wouldn't be enough creatures to control the plants from getting out of hand and feeding life into the soil through their excrement. One role is not more valuable than the other. Without balance, the forest suffers.

We see this necessity for balance reflected in our gardens, our relationships, our careers, our communities and ourselves. By nature, I am a giver. I love to nurture those around me, sometimes to the point of exhaustion. That is why, for how much I give, I must ensure I also take something for me, whatever that may look like. A day to rest, a trip, creating art, having a day of self-care—whatever it may be, I'm taking the day to care for myself. Oddly enough, even giving too much and overwhelming a situation can throw it out of balance, so it is important to establish boundaries as well. There is such a thing as overloving your plants. You don't want to overwater your garden and accidentally drown your crops! Learn to observe and know when enough is enough.

On the other end of the stick, you have moments when you can take too much. Mother Nature shows us it's important to respect the abundance that she shares, because we are not the only ones who are here to enjoy it. Sadly, it seems humanity has reached a point of such deep self-absorption that we've lost sight of all that is truly here. This is a world filled with trillions upon trillions of other creatures, and we must remember that we are sharing this planet with them. In our gardens, we have the opportunity to honor that relationship between us and the natural world. Our gardens teach us how to respectfully take, how to coexist, how to establish boundaries and how to give.

The abundance we are able to enjoy from our gardens is the result of all the hard work we must do to achieve it. When you work from a place of deep appreciation and gratitude for the land that you are able to steward, it builds a deep level of respect for the world around you. You see, the truth is, Mother Nature thrived for millions of years before us. She doesn't need us for her to thrive. In reality, we need her to sustain us, to feed us and to protect us. In our gardens, we can thank Mother Earth by giving what we can to nurture and honor her. For all that we take, we must also give. For every fruit harvested, we must renourish. For every seed planted, we must express our gratitude.

The way Mother Nature teaches us to care for her in a balanced way is how she teaches us to create balance in every aspect of our own lives as well. When you are tapped into the overflow of abundance that is available to you, when your cup is overflowing with love, it is so fulfilling to pour that love and abundance into the ones you love. Especially when in such alignment with yourself. When you continue to give, even after your own cup has been emptied, you can begin to harbor resentment because what you are giving is not reciprocated by those you are giving to. Giving to others does not obligate them to return that kindness. It's wonderful when they do, but it also has to be something you give to yourself. Relying on it from sources beyond yourself puts the power over your life in the hands of others. You must claim that power and learn to harness it within yourself.

To me, true success is being able to share an abundance cultivated from living my truth because I'm giving my most authentic self to the people around me. I have prioritized my divine self enough that it's able to shine its light into the lives of others. Because I have given to myself, I can now give to others in a way that doesn't deplete me. I have established a balance in my life between giving to myself and giving to others. In that balance, I find such a deep and profound state of peace. A peace that allows me to tap into the frequency of abundance whenever I please, because *my peace, my calm is orchestrating at the same wavelength of that abundance.* I know that the love I have for myself is infinite, so the love I have to share is infinite, so the abundance that I can cultivate in my life is infinite.

Cosmos in bloom, signaling the arrival of midsummer in the garden.

Chapter 2

Why Grow a Garden?

To get things started, I'd like to share with you why I find it so essential that we all try our best to grow a garden and connect with the natural world. I firmly believe that, through a deeper connection with Mother Earth, we can lead lives more in tune with ourselves and life's overflowing abundance.

I Am My Garden: Learning Self-Care

When I look at my garden, I see a reflection of myself. My garden mirrors not so much my physical appearance, but the state of my inner world. You see, our gardens, through the ways we tend to them, can show us the ways in which we must tend to ourselves. The responsibilities that are bestowed when you take on the role of a gardener are parallel to the responsibilities of loving yourself. The garden illuminates us on the importance of patience when focusing on these tasks. It can take time to get the job done, but do the work and you and the garden will become oh so abundant.

The way that we water our plants is the way we should pour into ourselves. We must fill our lives with joyful and fulfilling experiences. Just as our precious plants need water, we also need those moments of joy, laughter and excitement. A plant in the wild has no choice but to wait for rain. We've been gifted the ability to move, to take steps toward what we need and what we desire. Rarely do those moments simply find us, so we must take responsibility and actively search for the experiences that will fill our soul. If we go too long without watering ourselves, we will begin to wilt. There is an abundant life worth living and we owe it to ourselves to take that first step forward, even if we don't know where it will lead us.

As nice as it is to wake up early and quench the morning thirst of my garden, I must admit there is a wonderful relief when I wake up to the sounds of raindrops hitting the tin roof, pitter-pattering me back to sleep. I can rest easy knowing the plants aren't just getting watered, they're getting their absolute favorite drink. *Rain.* Drops of water that fall from the sky and deliver precious minerals. In our own lives, we may experience rainy days, moments when we feel overwhelmed, full of emotions that are pouring down and weighing on us. But within that rain are precious minerals, precious truths that are essential to our growth as well. It may not always feel the best, but it is okay not to be okay. Those negative emotions are just as much a part of us as the positive ones. Rather than push them away, we must tend to them, cradle them, and when possible, release them to make way for new streams to pour in that will help us grow. Even in the darkness, a seed will drink in the rain and sprout toward the sky.

The way the old leaves of plants die and must be pruned away is how we must let go of parts of ourselves that no longer serve us. It can be a hard truth to face. Those parts of ourselves, those beliefs, patterns or relationships that have carried us so far, have reached their peak and are now hindering our growth. Like a leaf, these parts of us can remain attached until something snips them away. It's a funny thing with humans. We're the ones that get attached. With plants, going too long without pruning these dying leaves can manifest as a variety of issues that can hinder the plants from growing to their fullest potential, such as by attracting disease or pests that feed on the decay. It may hurt the plants for a moment, but those leaves have to be let go.

Letting these things go can be as easy as snipping them clean off, but sometimes it can be painful, like slowly uprooting a weed that holds its grip deep beneath the soil. The longer we allow the weed to grow, the deeper its roots will anchor themselves, sucking more and more energy away the larger it gets. It can be incredibly challenging and time consuming, but once those final stringy roots are pulled from the world below, there is suddenly so much room to breathe. A relieving gasp of air that hasn't been felt in those dark depths for a very long time.

Corn seedlings breaching the soil, eager to grow.

The way a garden thrives when it is abundant and biodiverse is the way our communities, our societies and our civilizations can thrive when they are more connected and full of different individuals and ideas. Each individual flower in a biodiverse garden attracts different pollinators in the way that each unique individual attracts different ideas that can benefit the collective, ideas that other members could not have conceptualized simply because they come from their own unique path of experiences. The more life a garden attracts, the richer the quality of life becomes. If there is enough biodiversity in a garden, it will reach the point of becoming completely self-sustaining. It takes on a life of its own and thrives. The plants and wildlife synchronize and a beautiful hymn starts to play. The garden finds harmony. It may take some time, years even, but every plant and creature finds its special role to play in the collective abundance of the garden. If there is a lack of diversity in the garden, it leaves monocultures of plants vulnerable to other pests and conditions that other plants could have helped prevent by attracting and creating their own unique set of circumstances. If I plant a bed of just tomatoes, they'll become vulnerable to aphids. Aphids that nasturtiums could have helped manage, if planted in the vicinity, by attracting ladybugs that love to feed on those pesky pests. There is very little abundance without diversity.

So, you see, there are many parallels between plants and humans. It's important that we take the time to look in the mirror that is our garden and pay attention to what she can truly show us. Mother Nature is so gracious with her abundance that she even teaches us the way of cultivating it within ourselves. When we grow a garden, we learn the ways to grow ourselves.

The Nutritional Value

There is something truly magical about harvesting fresh food from your own garden. The flavor is brighter, the colors are more vibrant and the nutritional value is often far greater than what you would find in a grocery store. When you grow your own food, you have the power to choose the varieties that you love, to harvest them at the peak of ripeness and to enjoy them at their fullest potential. One of the key reasons that fresh, homegrown food is so nutritious is that it hasn't had to travel long distances or sit on a shelf for days or weeks. Many fruits and vegetables start to lose nutrients the moment they are harvested, and the longer they sit, the more nutrients they lose. But when you grow your own food, you can harvest it fresh off the vine and enjoy it when it's at its most nutritious.

Beyond growing for the nutritional benefits, cultivating your own food is a deeply nourishing experience for the soul. It allows you to slow down and connect with Nature in a way that is rare in our fast-paced, technology-driven world. You get to witness the magic of a tiny seed sprouting into a thriving plant, to feel the cool earth in your hands and the gentle touch of leaves on your skin, and to enjoy the delicious fruits of your labor in a way that is deeply fulfilling.

Cultivating your own abundance allows you to appreciate the hard work and effort that goes into producing the food that sustains us, something that our modern society has lost touch with. The fruit tastes so much sweeter, knowing how much love and hard work went into growing that food, especially when it's by your very hand.

Clean Food

We live in a world where food is more readily available than ever before. Grocery stores are filled to the brim with every imaginable product, from fresh produce to packaged snacks. But what many of us fail to consider is the true cost of this "abundance." Industrial agriculture has fundamentally altered the way we grow and produce our food, and the consequences of this transformation are gut wrenching.

To uphold this massive system, there is a relentless use of toxic and persistent chemicals to control the conditions needed to grow these foods. The chemicals employed in industrial agriculture are not just harmful to the environment; they are harmful to our health as well. Pesticides, herbicides and fertilizers can linger on our food, contaminating it with residues that can have serious negative impacts on our body over time. These chemicals are also harmful to the farmers and workers who come into contact with them regularly, as well as to the animals and ecosystems that are affected by their use.

A freshly harvested tomato, at peak nutritional value. >

This is where the act of growing our own food becomes truly radical. By choosing to cultivate our own gardens and grow our own food naturally, we are taking a stand against the destructive forces of industrial agriculture. We are reclaiming our power to make decisions about the food we eat and we are creating a healthier, more sustainable future for ourselves, our communities and our children.

Growing our own food in our gardens is an important step toward creating a more just and equitable food system. Industrial agriculture has created a food system that is heavily reliant on fossil fuels, monoculture crops and exploitative labor practices. This system prioritizes profit over people and the environment, and it perpetuates systemic inequality and food insecurity.

But by choosing to grow our own food and supporting local, sustainable agriculture, we can help create a more just and equitable food system. If you don't necessarily have access to growing your own, you can support small-scale farmers and producers who prioritize the health of our food, our environment and our communities. It is about taking a stand against the destructive forces of industrial agriculture and creating a more just and sustainable future for ourselves and our communities. It is about connecting with the natural world and cultivating a deeper appreciation for the food that sustains us.

The Power of Self-Sufficiency

In a world dominated by mass consumerism and on-grid living, gardening and growing your own food can be a revolutionary act of self-sufficiency. By cultivating your own fruits, vegetables and herbs, you take back control over your own food supply and become less reliant on a system that often prioritizes profit over health and sustainability.

Growing our own food allows us to step into one of the greatest powers we can have—the power to secure our own food supply. The recent pandemic showed us just how reliant we are on our food systems—so reliant that we've completely lost touch with how food is grown, where it comes from and what we're really consuming. When we personally grow the food that sustains us, we know all the love and hard work that goes into it. There's a deeper connection to our food, our planet and ourselves when we commit to cultivating such abundance.

Even greater, when you learn to grow so much abundance, you can tap into the power of community that it can foster. It's so rewarding to be able to grow such an overabundance that you're able to share with your loved ones, your friends or your neighbors. It gives you the opportunity to connect with others, to share your knowledge, your skills and your harvests with a community that allows everyone to thrive. If you don't necessarily have the access to space where you can grow your own food, you can help support your local food systems and reduce the carbon footprint by supporting local farms and markets.

Connecting with Nature: Learning Her Language

There is such a fulfillment when you're able to tune into the frequency of a garden and the natural world around you. It's a true wonder that somehow, without saying a single word, plants are able to communicate with the world around them in a way that so many creatures have come to understand so that they can acquire everything that they need. To a scientist, it's clear that they lure in those who they need to spread their pollen and seed through scent and color, but I am still left in complete awe at how plants even know to seek the assistance of something beyond themselves. To the naked eye, it seems like plants just sit there basking in the sun all day, but there is something far greater at work. Something we cannot see or hear. A language all their own.

Plants thrive because of the connections they have built within their environment, connections that are the result of millions of years of evolution. It is such an absolute marvel that we are all here in this very moment, this time, this era where we can witness the culmination of those millions of years of genetic variations that have led to what we are witnessing today. Do you understand that certain flowers are only the color that they are because that color attracts a very specific bird or insect to drink the nectar deep in its trumpet? Seemingly without the gift of sight, these plants have developed the exact sequences of DNA that manifests the color that they, themselves, cannot see to attract that which can. How does a plant know what color its flower needs to be? Does the bird whisper that its favorite color is red? Does the butterfly whisper that it sees only blue? I can't help but think that there is something far greater at play on this Earth. A language we cannot hear but that is so clearly present.

Although we ourselves cannot hear the frequencies at which these plants speak, they still find a way to show us their truth. If we want a lesson in honesty, we should spend time with a plant. For us to understand the language of plants, at least the one we can comprehend, all we have to do is be present and pay attention. Plants will unapologetically tell us if they aren't happy in a myriad of ways. If they are parched, they begin to wilt. If their leaves begin to yellow, perhaps they are lacking proper nutrition. When a plant in the shadows crawls toward the light, perhaps they need more sun. Plants may not speak, but they most definitely have plenty to say. All we have to do is take the time to learn their language.

Chapter 3

What to Know Before Starting a Garden

I wish I could experience the creation of my garden for the first time all over again. It may have been immensely overwhelming, but that sense of whimsy, excitement and discovery at every turn is a feeling I can only relive in my memory. It's a feeling so pure and childlike that I've only ever felt in my garden.

Of course, the discoveries in the garden are never ending, but there's something about doing it for the first time that makes your heart flutter, like falling in love for the first time. Now that my fingers are familiar with the stains of tomato leaves and the garden breathes a life of its own, I can look back at all the things I wish I knew before breaking ground for the first time. I've divided this chapter into digestible sections so you can better understand what to think about before getting your hands dirty.

What Is the Intention of Your Garden?

Gardens can serve so many purposes. They can bring us endless joy with their beautifully curated naturescape; they can provide us with delicious bounty to nourish our body and soul; they can provide solace and opportunity for local wildlife. The real question is, what do *you* want to achieve in your garden?

The magic of a garden is that it could actually fulfill all these purposes all at once. The decision is ultimately yours and what you want your dream garden to be. Let's try something for a moment.

Take a deep breath and close your eyes. Imagine yourself at the center of your dream garden. What does it look like? What do you hear? What do you smell? As you're walking through, do you feel the soft brush of leaves on your fingertips? Do you feel the sun's rays kissing your skin as it dapples through the trees? Or are you entranced by the symphony of buzzing bees feeding on the sweet nectar of flowers? Is there juice running down your lip from the freshly plucked tomato you just bit into? What do you see?

Now, open your eyes.

Knowing the intention of your garden will not only help you envision all the possibilities in your garden, it'll inspire you to do it.

Depending on your intention, you will begin to learn exactly what you need to do to build the garden of your dreams. For example, if you want to curate a natural landscape of native plants to encourage your native wildlife, you may be able to plant directly into your native soil with some light amendments and work organically with the shapes of your space. If you want to plant a few trees to create shade for you and a home for birds, you know you'll need ample space to do so. If you want to plant vegetables but your soil is too sandy, you can build raised beds and add your own garden soil. There are so many possibilities; it's just about what you desire.

Learning Your Conditions

Step 1: Understanding Your Hardiness Zone

Before even thinking about what you *want* to grow, you need to have a richer understanding of what you can grow by learning about your climate. In the world of gardening, we break down regions into something called hardiness zones, also known as your growing zones. Your hardiness zone defines your average annual minimum temperatures, which is essential to determining what plants can grow in your area. In the United States, they range from zones 1 to 13, 1 being the coldest of climates and 13 being the warmest. Typically, the lower zones have a longer winter period, whereas the highest zones hardly experience the cold, if at all. That winter period plays a significant role in the types of plants you will be able to grow and will also determine the best time for you to start a garden.

< A rare glimpse of the very beginning stages of the vegetable garden, March 2020. Everything I explain in this chapter is what I wish I knew before getting started. In our excitement, we just picked up our shovels and started digging.

To give you an example, my gardens are located in central Tennessee, which falls right in between hardiness zones 7 and 8. It's easy to find on a hardiness map, but for an exact zone, I simply searched my zip code's hardiness zone online. I am in growing zone 7b, which means I can grow plants that have a hardiness that reaches down to zone 7. When acquiring or researching plants, the zones they grow well in are usually listed on their description or label.

Hardiness zones are important to understand because you want to ensure you're growing plants that will actually thrive in your climate. It's possible to grow warmth-loving plants in lower zones if you have a place to protect them indoors throughout the winter. If you try growing a plant that thrives in zones 2 to 5 in a warm zone like 9 or 10, it's very unlikely that plant will thrive, or it will take a significant amount of extra attention to ensure its survival.

Once you understand your growing zone, you can start compiling a list of everything you can actually grow in your climate. This applies to all types of plants, whether you're wanting to grow vegetables, flowers or trees. Local nurseries typically stock plants that would do well in your area, but if you're ordering your plants online, do a little bit of extra research to ensure it's suitable for your area. A quick internet search that helped me when I was getting started was, "What vegetables can grow in zone 7?"

Step 2: Finding Your Light

Every single plant on Earth needs light to grow, some a little more or a little less than others. It is so important that you understand what kind of light your growing space gets and how it travels throughout the day. This will help you determine what kind of plants will flourish in your space.

To do this, you can go outside to your desired growing space at different times throughout the day to see how the sun shines through the area. I'd go out every hour or two and take note of how the light is traveling through your space. Pay attention to any shadows being cast by neighboring buildings or trees.

The light requirement of plants can be broken down into three simple categories: full sun, part sun and full shade. When researching plants or shopping at a local nursery, most labels will state the plants' lighting needs. Plants that require full sun need at least six hours of direct sunlight to thrive; part sun plants do well in four to six hours of full sunlight; and full shade plants require a shady area out of direct sunlight. Plants have developed their specific lighting requirement through their evolutionary needs in the wild. When I am researching a plant, I like to think about where it usually grows in the wild—does it like to grow in sunny grasslands, shady canopies of the forest or alongside rivers? Understanding where plants grow in the wild helps us understand how we can meet those environmental needs in our own gardens.

How the shade casted from a tree changes throughout the day.

Something important to note as well, is that as the seasons change, so does the direction of sunlight. For example, in early spring, the sun travels closer to the horizon and casts different layers of shade in the garden, but during the midsummer months, the sun travels directly overhead with a new pattern of shadows underneath.

With an understanding of how the light travels through your space and how much light is available to you, you can really narrow down the list of plants that you wish to grow. Many people think that if they have a shady space, they can't grow much, but you'd be surprised how many plants would actually thrive with less direct sunlight.

Step 3: **Assess Your Soil**

Soil is the foundation for all life that grows on Earth, so it's especially important to understand what kind of soil you have in your space. In future chapters, we will talk about ways you can amend your soil, but to get things started, just get out there and dig a small hole so you know what you're working with.

Is your soil dense red clay? Is it rocky or sandy? How well does it hold moisture? I know many growers who take it as far as mailing out samples to be tested for a complete breakdown of their soil. This is great for learning the level of acidity and nutrients that exists in your soil. The deeper

an understanding you have of your soil, the better equipped you'll be in knowing how to properly amend it so that whatever you plant can grow to its fullest potential. Having this knowledge will also help you determine what kind of beds you would like to create for your plants. If your soil is too sandy or very rocky, it may be best to pursue raised beds. If you have red clay, you could follow the path of amending your soil and creating allotments right in the ground.

When assessing your soil, this is also a great time to learn about the native plants in your area. If you want to plant an ornamental garden or pollinator-friendly plants, introducing native species is a great way to invigorate the local wildlife while also curating a space that's much easier to manage. You see, native plants have a much better time acclimating to the native soil in your space because they have evolved to thrive there.

In later chapters, we will dive deeper into how you can amend your soil and preserve the ecology within it as well, but as an introduction, I want to plant this seed in your mind: The most important thing we can do for our soil is protect the ecology within it.

Special note: When you're assessing your soil, it's also a great time to learn whether you have any existing water or gas pipes, or electrical cables, running through your growing space.

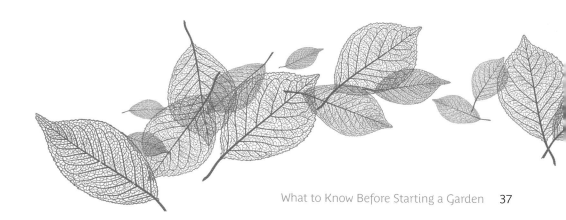

The Blue Bellflower

Step 4: Pay Attention to the Water

Before planting anything in the garden, it's essential to understand what your moisture conditions are. Does it rain a lot in your area? Does it pool in certain areas of your yard?

Unless you're going to build some type of shelter for your plants, it can be challenging trying to control how the rain affects them. If you live in an area more prone to rain, think about planting plants that enjoy that much moisture and will have no trouble with all the rain. If you live in an area with less rain, think about plants that are a bit more drought tolerant.

Inevitably, whether you experience a lot of rain or not, there will be times when you can't rely on Mother Nature to meet the watering needs of all your plants. Every plant needs a certain amount of water to thrive, so make sure you have access to water, whether it's through a spigot, a well or a rain catchment system (please make sure rain catchment is legal in your area before pursuing).

Rainwater is the absolute best for plants but if you can't easily access it during drier periods, use what you have available to you. If you're pulling water from a city line or even a well, I would recommend attaching a filter to your spigot to clean out any extra sediment or chemicals in the water.

One of many joys of gardening is being able to spend time in it every single day, nurturing and caring for all your plants. But in reality, not many of us have the luxury of spending as much time as we'd like in the garden to care for our plants the way they need, especially when it comes to watering. I have a fairly large garden and I'm fortunate to have the time to care for it on a daily basis so I can go through and hand water my plants individually. If you don't have the luxury of time, think about ways you can care for your garden when you aren't there by setting up an irrigation system with a timer.

Step 5: How Much Space Do You Have?

Space may very well be the most valuable resource you have because, once you start planting, you'll just want to plant more and more. So, it's important to have an understanding of what you want to grow and how to make the best use of your space to grow it.

When researching plants or shopping around at a local garden center, pay attention to how much room the plant you're desiring needs to grow to its full potential. Not just that, but think about how it would influence other plants neighboring it. For example, if you want to incorporate a plant with big leaves and tall flowers, consider the shade it will cast over other plants. Will it affect their growth or will you plant something that will appreciate the added shade? Also, how wide will that flowering plant grow to be? It's very possible it can smother other plants close by if planted too close. Or what if you wanted to plant a tree? That will definitely require a good amount of space, but the shady area it casts underneath may be perfect for some shade-loving plants.

There's also the potential of planting things vertically as well, either on a trellis or on a fence. Planting vertically is an amazing way to maximize space and add a beautiful new layer to the garden.

Ultimately, understand that every single thing that you plant will have an effect on your space and on other plants. Every decision you make counts.

Another thing to keep in mind when thinking about utilizing your space is to give yourself room to maneuver through the garden with tools and large pots. How will you balance the use of negative space and garden?

Step 6: Get Familiar with Your Local Wildlife

Inevitably, the moment you plant something in your garden, it will begin to attract something, such as pollinators, pests, small mammals and birds. Before getting anything in the ground, it's important to learn the local fauna so that you can set up your garden for success right from the start. Something that we must really be conscious of is that every single decision we make in the garden will have some sort of influence on other plants and creatures.

How will you incorporate certain features and maintain your garden so that it's working as harmoniously with your local landscape as possible? Will you introduce a few birdbaths so that wildlife can feel welcomed and find an oasis in your space? Will you introduce native flowers or berries into your space to encourage your local creatures? Can you build special cages to protect certain crops from unwanted pests, rather than using harsh chemicals? This is the time to think about these questions, so you are prepared for whatever may come in the future.

This is also a great time to illuminate yourself on companions within the garden that can help redirect unwanted visitors without having to use harmful chemicals or taking drastic action. We will speak more deeply on companion plants in another chapter, but know that the greatest way to create a healthy and naturally attuned garden is through the use of companions. I've even seen people go as far as planting sacrificial plants meant to lure visitors right to it and away from your precious plants.

Deciding What to Grow

Upon doing all the research that goes into learning your conditions, you may have been faced with some hard truths. Sometimes, we end up in situations where our conditions just aren't suitable for some of the plants we want to grow. But that's okay because we've also learned about all the amazing plants that we *can* grow! If you're anything like me, you'll even push the boundaries of a plant's growing zone just a tad if you absolutely can't live without it in the garden. If you have access to a greenhouse or somewhere where you could store plants for the winter, you can even pull up the more sensitive plants before frost or during dormancy so you can replant them in the spring. *The things we do for plants!*

If you're as eager as me, there's only so much research I can really sit down and try to learn before I have the urge to get out there and start planting. The best way to learn about your conditions is to *experience* them for yourself. Allow yourself to become limitless and plant everything your heart desires. Witness for yourself what plants thrive in your conditions and what plants you need to do more preparation for. Learn along the way, unshrouded by the fear of failure. It's okay if things don't necessarily go as planned. If we have learned something, it was worth it.

For this part, I wanted to walk through my process of determining what to grow in a new space. I'll show you how I use the steps to decide on what I can grow. Let's set the scene:

The space I'm working with is a slightly overgrown backyard. It's been given enough attention over the years to have some shape and an established 20-foot (about 6-m) maple tree in the far right corner. As soon I walk through the sliding door, I'm welcomed by a small but comfortable paved patio space about 5 feet (about 1.5 m) long and the full width of my fenced yard. Walking forward, I can follow a cement paved pathway about 20 feet down to a tall wooden fence—a wood that was once stained a dark walnut but has faded from years in the sun. It lines the entirety of the yard. On the left of the walkway, I have space slightly smaller than the side on the right. The winters can be long, but spring is cool and moist. Summers are hot and humid, fall subdues it quickly.

Let's say I just moved in and I see this not-too-shabby green space in the back. One of the main reasons I chose this place was because of the potential to grow my own food in the backyard, something I never really had the space to do. I've never grown anything before, so I'm breaking soil for the first time.

It's midfall. I've just read *Gardening for Abundance* and I'm inspired to learn about all the possibilities I have in these conditions. (Please don't mind the shameless self-promotion.) Anyway, following the steps in "Learning Your Conditions" (page 35), the first thing I need to do is research my *growing zone*. The first gusts of winter start creeping in around the end of October, but I have no idea what that means for the plants. I search for my zone online, type in my zip code, and I learn I'm in growing zone 6. I type into my phone, "What can I grow in growing zone 6?" A long list of veggies, herbs, flowers, shrubs and trees appears on the screen. I'm overwhelmed but

The first flower buds of midsummer. >

I'm so happy to see that I can grow tomatoes! That's one I was really hoping for; they're one of my favorites in the kitchen.

Before I get too ahead of myself, I need to think about my intentions for this garden. I know I want to grow food, so I'm going to dedicate a lot of space to that. I'd also love to help my local pollinators by sprinkling in a few varieties of flowers. Space is limited, so shrubs aren't the top of the priority list, especially with a beautiful maple already planted. I close my eyes and envision the dazzling show it'll give in the fall with its changing leaves. What an amazing element to have in the garden.

My mind is set: I'm going to create a proper kitchen garden full of veggies and herbs, with light sequences of florals for the bees. Now, I need to see how light travels through

An abundant tomato harvest. Varieties featured: Costoluto Fiorentino, Marsalato, Cherokee Purple and Oxheart.

my space. I'm up early, just past eight. With a fresh cup of tea in hand, I step outside to observe how the light enters my space. In the distance to the east, there is a long row of tall shrubs a neighbor planted as a windbreak. The sun is just starting to peek over them. My green space is still in the shade, noticeably moist from the morning dew. The right wall of the fence is bright, receiving the first rays of sunlight in the backyard. I head back in. At around two hours later, I head back out and see most of the right side of my space is fully illuminated by the sun. Good thing it's a sunny day, perfect for observation. Based on what I'm seeing, I already know the right side of the garden will be getting a good amount of sunlight. I make a note and head back in. A work call drags on longer than expected, so I don't make it out again until around one p.m. The entire backyard is illuminated, but there's a heavy contrast under the tree. It's casting quite a bit of shade directly underneath and a little bit into the space in front of it. I don't think plants that need a lot of sunlight would do so well under there, but maybe some shade lovers can thrive. I make a note and whip up some lunch. It's a quarter to four and I head back out. The tree's shadow has swayed farther to the left and is now shading the walkway. Only a part of the left green space is shaded and most of the right is still beaming. The fence begins casting a sharp line of shade. The air is cool. I pull up a sun chair and watch the evening set in. As the hours pass, I watch the tree's shadow glide across the ground until it meets the eastern fence. The right side is slowly falling under the rising shade of the western wall. By sunset, I have observed that the right area gets the most sunlight, but the left holds up well through the second half

of the day. I don't see the path of the tree's shadow being as obstructive as the shade directly below it, so the potential to grow an abundance of plants is still there.

Now for the fun part. It's time to get my hands dirty. I must assess the soil. With my trowel, I pierce the Earth for the first time. I pay attention to how it felt pushing through the soil. Was it hard on impact, or did it slide in smoothly? Was there a crunch from the blade striking stone? Searching for any hints of what lies below, I slowly place the first scoopful in my hand, gently tilting it to the side for revelation. The soil is cool to the touch from a faintness of moisture. It holds some water, but it is still brittle and crumbling in my hand. There is a denseness to it and some noticeable weight in my hand. As I crumble it in my hands, little bits mush against my skin, staining them a reddish brown. It feels as though, if it got wet, it would slosh around in my hand. I lean in so it can meet my nose. A deep earthy scent with a hint of grass after it rains. I poke a few times into the small hole I dug. It is pretty compact and takes a few jabs to really break it down. On the bright side, it seems to hold quite a bit of moisture. Plant roots can manage well in silty clay soil, but I wonder whether there's anything I can add to loosen it up a bit. Add some texture. Nonetheless, there's potential. I also take a look under the tree to see how the soil is there. It's noticeably drier, probably because of the tree drinking its large fill and blocking rainfall. Either I plant plants that can handle drier shade, or I amend the soil to better hold moisture.

Feeling the dryness of the soil reminds me of the next step. Water. I look up at the sky and wonder about the rainfall. Does it not rain often? Does it rain too much? What are my water sources? Plants need moisture, so I have to make sure they all have access to water. Luckily there's a spigot, but plants really like rainwater, so it wouldn't hurt to have a catchment around. If my work schedule picks up, will I be able to keep up with watering? Maybe I can set up irrigation so the plants can get watered even if I'm not around as often.

I head down the path to the patio and take a good look at the space. The possibilities take form in my mind as I process the layout and what I've just learned. It's about a 12 x 20-foot (about 3.7 x 6-meter) space, so there's lots of room to work with. How much space do I want to dedicate to beds? Do I want long, wide beds or smaller, more organized ones? What's the vibe I'm going for? How much space will the plants I want to grow need? To get the most out of my planting, it's essential to think of ways to maximize the space.

As I'm envisioning, I see a squirrel scurry across the yard and up the maple tree. What other little furry or feathered friends are living around here? I don't want to disturb their peace, so I start thinking of ways to protect my plants without disrupting their daily life. I can place a birdbath to help them feel welcomed, hang a few feeders so they have their own source of food away from my veggies. I do a quick search and learn that cabbage worms are a serious issue for growers in the area, so I think about building small mesh cages for the cauliflower I want to grow. To maximize my space, I'm also thinking about ways of interplanting certain plants to both benefit pollinators and repel any unwanted critters.

Things have really come together and I have a much clearer picture of what I'm working with in my growing space. Now, it's time to think about gathering the materials to make it happen. What do I need and where can I get it? Fortunately, the soil has immense potential for things to grow, so I'm thinking about planting directly into the ground by creating allotments. To help the soil loosen up and aerate some more, I may mix in some sand as I'm amending the bed. I like the look of a wild garden, so planting directly in the soil will be aesthetically pleasing and also more cost effective. Raised beds can be pricey, depending on the material they're made with. I can slowly incorporate raised beds over the years if I really want to, but to get things going sooner, I'm working with what I got. To work as harmoniously with the land as possible, I'll be applying the no-till gardening method (see page 55) rather than tilling and disturbing the soil. I'll only have to dig up a few older root systems, but everything else can stay intact. I will have my beds slightly organized with pathways in between, but they'll be fairly large beds. I'm going to need quite a bit of soil to get the garden started. I call up a few of the local garden centers and they have garden soil and compost available to purchase in bulk. Now that I know how I'm going to be building my beds, it's time to think of everything I want to grow and how it'll all fill the space. I want the ideal kitchen garden. I want fresh tomatoes, peppers, corn, leafy greens, beans, rosemary, thyme, lavender, oregano, onions, carrots, cauliflower, kale and squash. I'd love to intermingle some coneflowers, coreopsis and sunflowers, too, for the pollinators. To get the most out of my space, I'd like to have a trellis or two in place for some of my vining growers, such as squash.

Now, with a firm understanding of my conditions and everything I want to grow, it's time to make a *garden plan*.

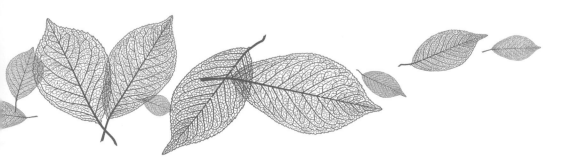

Chapter 4

Making a Garden Plan

Now that we have some insight on what we should know before starting a garden, we can really start to narrow down what we want to grow and how to transform our space to grow it! One of my absolute favorite projects within gardening is drawing up a *garden plan*.

A garden plan is an invaluable resource that will help you manifest the garden of your dreams! Essentially, it's a layout of what you want your garden design to look like, accompanied by a list of all the plants you want to grow. This is the time for you to think as far out of the box as you want and brainstorm. I prefer to do this over the winter months; it's a great way to give yourself the time you need to really prepare. Not to mention, it really pulls me out of my gloomy slump. Allow me to guide you through the steps I take to draw up my own garden plan.

By this point, I would hope that you've become very familiar with your space and your conditions. With that knowledge, you should have a much better idea of what you hope to grow in your garden. To get things started, I lace up my winter boots and head to the garden with a sketchbook in hand. I breathe in the cool air, close my eyes, and prepare my mind for all the possibilities.

Now I already have an established garden, but every year brings about change. I start by sketching out the shapes of the garden beds that I know I'll be keeping throughout the season. Nothing too refined, just simple loose lines to get the layout going. Get as messy and wild as you want, let your hand flow across the paper without hesitation. When starting from scratch, this is a fun time in visualizing the shapes of your garden. Do you want round beds or something more organized? Visualize the pathways you see yourself walking through as you navigate through your space. While doing this, equip yourself with a lengthy tape measure, so you can also start getting an idea of the exact dimensions of your beds as well. Precise measurements of beds will come in handy when it comes time to curate the plants that'll be going in. The size of the bed is really up to you and the space you're working in. I have a wide variety of beds in my garden in a range of different sizes and shapes. Some beds are 6 x 8 feet (about 1.8 x 2.4 m), some are 4 x 16 feet (about 1.2 x 4.9 m) and I even have a massive plot in the far back of the garden that's roughly 8 x 20 feet (about 2.4 x 6.1 m). Again, it's all about what you want your space to look like.

During this initial sketch, it's also helpful to make note of the existing structures in the space, such as trees or walkways. Also, don't forget about growing vertically as well, it's an amazing way to maximize space. When I first started my garden, I was fortunate enough to not have any major obstacles in my way, so the brainstorm was very free flowing and I didn't have to think about working around anything. A few years later, I now have established trees and very solid beds, so any additions I want to make in the garden have to have those existing structures in mind. In this brainstorming stage, I'm sure not to rush myself, drawing up a few variations of how I want the structure of the garden to look before making any final decisions. I keep the plants I want to grow in mind as I envision the amount of space I can give them to make them feel right at home.

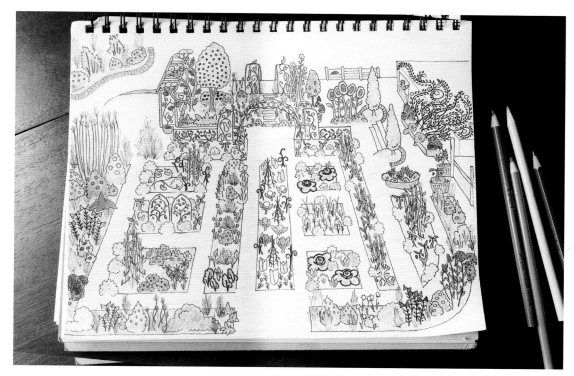

The illustration of the Redleaf 2023 Garden Plan.

Once you have the rough blueprint of your garden sketched out, it's time to define your lines and get a solid map made. With over a decade of experience with Adobe Photoshop, I like to digitize my map so I can easily print out blank copies to work with. You can also grab a ruler or compass to draw out your straight lines or perfectly rounded circles. You can make your garden plan as detailed and precise as you'd like. The more precise it is, the more of an idea you'll have of just how many plants you'll need to acquire to fill your space.

With a solid map of the garden made, I print out a blank copy and start playing around with different combinations of plants in each bed I've laid out. At this stage, I simply write the names of the plants I want to grow in each bed, researching their compatibility along the way. For example, if I want tomatoes in a bed, I need to make sure that any other plants that I pair alongside them will either benefit or at least not hinder their growth. This is a great time to reiterate any vertical structures you'd want to implement as well. Tomatoes can get very leggy, so I'm always sure to have a trellis in place wherever they're growing. In the early stages, the idea for what I want to plant is very broad. Once I finalize what I'm growing in a bed, I start to hone in on the exact proportions of the bed and how much space the specific plant I'm growing will need.

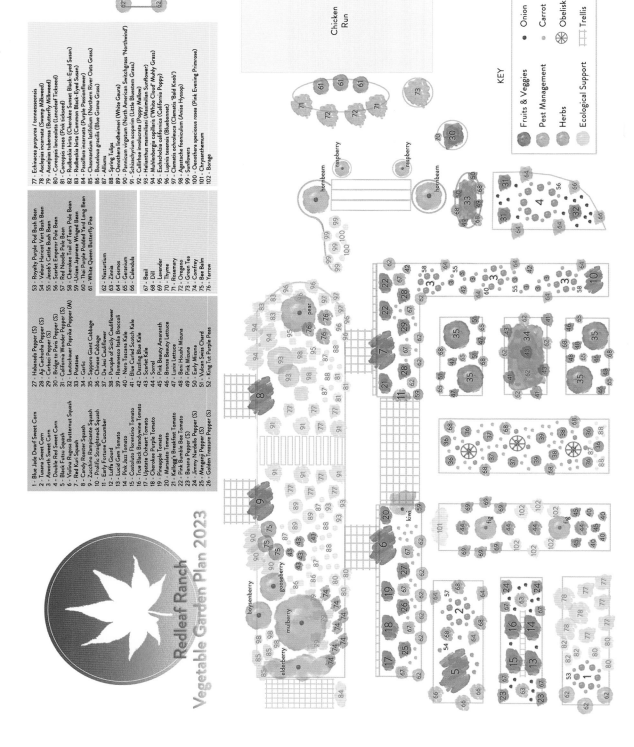

Redleaf Ranch Vegetable Garden Plan 2023

1 - Blue Jade Dwarf Sweet Corn
2 - Tuxana Sweet Corn
3 - Ashworth Sweet Corn
4 - Double Red Sweet Corn
5 - Black Futsu Squash
6 - Violina Rugosa Butternut Squash
7 - Red Kuri Squash
8 - Candy Roaster Squash
9 - Zucchino Rampicante Squash
10 - Prolific Straightneck Squash
11 - Early Fortune Cucumber
12 - Luffa Gourd
13 - Lucid Gem Tomato
14 - Pink Jazz Tomato
15 - Costoluto Fiorentino Tomato
16 - True Black Brandywine Tomato
17 - Upstate Oxheart Tomato
18 - Cherokee Purple Tomato
19 - Pineapple Tomato
20 - Marsalato Tomato
21 - Kellogg' Breakfast Tomato
22 - Pink Bumble Bee Tomato
23 - Banana Pepper (S)
24 - Jimmy Nardello Pepper (S)
25 - Manganji Pepper (S)
26 - Golden Treasure Pepper (S)

27 - Habanada Pepper (S)
28 - Aji Cachucha Pepper (S)
29 - Corbaci Pepper (S)
30 - Bridge to Paris Pepper (S)
31 - California Wonder Pepper (S)
32 - Leutschauer Paprika Pepper (M)
33 - Potatoes
34 - Garlic
35 - Sapporo Giant Cabbage
36 - Chinese Cabbage
37 - De Jesi Cauliflower
38 - Purple of Sicily Cauliflower
39 - Romanesco Italia Broccoli
40 - Nero Toscana Kale
41 - Blue Curled Scotch Kale
42 - Dazzling Blue Kale
43 - Scarlet Kale
44 - Sorrel
45 - Pink Beauty Amaranth
46 - Bronze Beauty Lettuce
47 - Lunix Lettuce
48 - Beni Houshi Mizuna
49 - Pink Mizuna
50 - Early Mizuna
51 - Vulcan Swiss Chard
52 - King Tut Purple Peas

53 - Royalty Purple Pod Bush Bean
54 - Velour Haricot Vert Bush Bean
55 - Jacob's Cattle Bush Bean
56 - Scarlet Emperor Pole Bean
57 - Red Noodle Pole Bean
58 - Cherokee Trail of Tears Pole Bean
59 - Urizen Japanese Winged Bean
60 - Thai Purple Podded Yard Long Bean
61 - White Queen Butterfly Pea

62 - Nasturtium
63 - Zinnia
64 - Cosmos
65 - Geranium
66 - Calendula

67 - Basil
68 - Dill
69 - Lavender
70 - Thyme
71 - Rosemary
72 - Oregano
73 - Green Tea
74 - Comfrey
75 - Bee Balm
76 - Yarrow

77 - Echinacea purpurea / tenneessensis
78 - Asclepias incarnata (Swamp Milkweed)
79 - Asclepias tuberosa (Butterfly Milkweed)
80 - Coreopsis lanceolata (Lanceleaf Tickseed)
81 - Coreopsis rosea (Pink tickseed)
82 - Rudbeckia hirta (Cherokee Sunset Black-Eyed Susan)
83 - Rudbeckia hirta (Common Black-Eyed Susan)
84 - Passiflora incarnata (Purple Passionflower)
85 - Chasmanthium latifolium (Northern River Oats Grass)
86 - Bouteloua gracilis (Blue Grama Grass)
87 - Alliums
88 - Spring Tulips
89 - Oenothera lindheimeri (White Gaura)
90 - Panicum virgatum (North American Switchgrass 'Northwind')
91 - Schizachyrium scoparium (Little Bluestem Grass)
92 - Callirhoe involucrata (Poppy Mallow)
93 - Helianthus maximiliani (Maximilian Sunflower)
94 - Muhlenbergia capillaris ('White Cloud' Muhly Grass)
95 - Eschscholzia californica (California Poppy)
96 - Lupinis texensis (Bluebonnet)
97 - Clematis ochroleuca (Clematis 'Bald Knob')
98 - Agastache foeniculum (Anise Hyssop)
99 - Sunflowers
100 - Oenothera speciosus rosea (Pink Evening Primrose)
101 - Chrysanthemum
102 - Borage

KEY

Fruits & Veggies
Pest Management
Herbs
Ecological Support

• Onion
Carrot
Obelisk
Trellis

Chicken Run

I should mention that there is lots of online software that will help you curate your gardens. Once you have your exact layout and dimensions solidified, they're a great resource to help you lay out your plants precisely. I'm an artist at heart, so I like to curate my own designs, adding a special touch to everything I do. Now that you have a clearer idea of what plants are going in each bed, you can start mapping out exactly how many plants will go into the beds and how you will interplant them. This is especially important if you're starting your plants from seed because it'll create a clear picture of how many plants you need to get started. Or if you're anything like me, you get an abundance of plants started just for the fun of it, and figure it all out later. I'm giving you the tools to set your garden up as precisely as you'd like, but ultimately the journey you take in your garden is up to you.

While I fill in my plan, I can't help but think about all the curveballs nature will throw my way during the season. No matter how well we plan things, we can never be too sure of what Mother Nature's plans are. One of the great joys of gardening is orchestrating a symphony of our own creation, but we must remember that plants, the wind, the rain, the beetles, the birds, and the bees all have a mind of their own. We can plan, we plant, we can nurture, but always count on nature to get involved. In our gardens, we also have a special opportunity to witness how plants influence each other. I may have a picture of how the plants will grow in my mind, but they always find a way to surprise me.

The final step to my own garden planning is completely optional, but I find it to be a powerful way to manifest a garden of abundance. We are vessels of creativity. Our creative energy is at its highest when we get creative, so I like to take my garden plan a step further by illustrating it. In the midst of visualizing my garden plan, I can close my eyes and see the garden in my mind. But like our thoughts, getting the visuals onto paper can bring more clarity and excitement. That is, of course, if our eyes agree with what they see drawn before them. Regardless of your artistic ability, the goal of illustrating is simply to enjoy it. Bask in the thought of all the abundance your garden will grow and create while intoxicated with that energy.

In the winter months, the creative process of creating my garden plan does a great job of lifting my spirits. Nothing warms me more than the hope of abundance right around the corner. Why not start harnessing that energy with a fun outlet? Better yet, I'll hit the ground running when it's time to break ground. When the days are longer and the soil is warmer, we'll be ready to build the garden of our dreams. At the peak of the season, I can't wait to hold up my plan next to the garden to see just how well I brought my vision to life. *Abundance.*

< *The Redleaf Ranch 2023 Garden Plan designed in Photoshop. While there are many garden design programs out there, I used Photoshop to create my blueprint.*

Chapter 5

Building the Foundation for Your Garden

With a deep understanding of your local conditions, a list of the plants you want to grow and your garden plan fully mapped out, it is finally time to start building your garden! In this chapter, I want to give you insight on the best time to start a garden and a few different methods for creating space for your plants.

The Best Time to Start a Garden

It's never too late to start a garden, but knowing the best time to build your foundation will set your plants up for success. Timing will vary, depending on your zone, but generally, in cooler climates, the best time to build your foundation would be in the fall or early spring. What it ultimately comes down to is your preparedness and your pace. Mind you, we're talking about *building the foundation*, not planting. We'll cover that soon.

Fall is a wonderful time to start building the foundation for a garden. The air is getting cool and it's far more pleasant to work outside. If you get your foundation ready before winter, you'll save yourself a lot of time in the spring, which can be directed to adding final amendments and actually planting your seedlings. If you aren't necessarily ready to completely build out the design for your garden, this is when to prepare the areas that you know you'll be growing in. If you have an area overrun with other plants, you can lay down a covering to kill them off throughout the winter. If you're in a warmer climate, you can also do this and allow it to break down the top layer of plants for at least three months before getting the framework in. This way, when it comes time to break ground, you'll have a nutrient-rich base ready to go. You can also prepare a space prior to planting by practicing the no-till gardening method, which I'll cover shortly. Essentially, what you're doing is sustainably preparing space by killing off plants you don't want in that space and adding a thick layer of amendments for the plants to grow in.

In early spring, you're more than welcome to build your foundation then, but you'll be a bit more pressed for time, depending on how quickly the growing climate rolls in. If you've prepared beforehand, you'll be able to focus more on amending and preparing the soil for your plants. Personally, I like to space out my tasks so I can give my best to each, rather than overwhelming myself with too much at once.

All that said, the best time to actually plant would be early to midspring, depending on the variety of plants. For plants that prefer cooler weather, you want to get them started as soon as the soil is workable and temperatures are consistently around 50°F (10°C). Plants that are frost hardy can endure the frost for some periods of time, but too much of it can stunt their growth, especially when they're delicate seedlings. Warmer growing plants can only go out into the garden once the risk of frost has completely passed in your area, typically around midspring. Any exposure to frost can severely damage young seedlings, significantly stunting their growth or even killing them.

Spring is also the ideal season to plant because cooler temperatures and more frequent rains are the perfect conditions for seedlings to get established. You definitely don't want your seedlings getting too dry or hot during these tender stages. If you plant seedlings in the heat of the summer, it'll take a significant amount of watering and extra care to make sure they pull through. Even then, you'll miss out on precious time needed for the plants to grow and provide you with anything worth harvesting. If planted in the spring, you'll have that much more time for plants to reach maturity and start producing their abundance in the summer.

If you want to grow plants from seed, make sure they are well suited for transplanting. Certain plants have very delicate root systems and can experience shock when removed from the pot and planted in the garden. For hardier plants, seedlings can be started indoors six to eight weeks before transplanting them outside. For us here in Tennessee, our plantings happen in two waves. The first wave is our cool crops in early spring, which is usually around mid-March. That means our seedlings were started six to eight weeks before setting them out, in mid-January. Our second wave is our hot crops, which get planted in mid-April when the risk of our last frost has passed. These seedlings were started in mid-February, six to eight weeks before transplanting them in the garden. When it comes to planting, timing is key so your seedlings are set up for success during the growing season. As for direct sowing seeds in the garden, the same system applies for cool crops and hot crops: Cool crops are sown in early spring and the hot crops are sown after the risk of frost.

If you rely more on acquiring seedlings from garden centers throughout the season, make sure you're aware of the plants' needs and the best time for planting. The best time to plant is most certainly in the spring. If you plant during summertime, you'll need to make sure you're watering plants frequently so they can endure the heat without drying out. Even then, the heat can significantly stress out any transplants and make it difficult for them to establish. If you have a long enough fall season to grow crops, seedlings are usually transplanted two to three months before your first frost, right around the end of summer.

With an understanding of the proper timing for preparing a garden and setting out plants for the growing season, you should have a better idea of when to get things started so that you can properly pace yourself. It can be overwhelming trying to get a garden ready while caring for seedlings all at once, so spacing things out can definitely help lighten the load.

Now that we've talked about timing, let's dive into how to prepare space for your plants. At the end of the day, the way you want your garden to look and feel is completely up to you and your needs. You can create allotments directly in the soil or curate something more structured with raised beds. No matter what vibe you're going for, the most effective and sustainable way to create a foundation for your plants is through no-till gardening (page 55).

Acquiring Resources

One of the biggest deterrents of those wanting to start a garden is cost. Here's the thing about your garden: The initial startup cost may be high, depending on how far you want to take it, but it's an investment in your overall well-being and future. After a few years, the reward far surpasses what you put in. Many people think it's expensive to set up a garden, but truthfully, it is only as pricey as you want it to be. There are many cost-effective ways to start building your beds; all that matters is how determined you are to create your garden.

From the start, I think the most costly elements that you'll need to invest in are garden soil and its amendments. Depending on the style of bed that you're looking for, that will determine how much soil you'll really need. The least expensive way to get soil is in bulk from local garden or horticulture centers. A few factors affect the price: your location, the amount, and the kind of amendments you want. To get a good bed going, you'll want garden soil and compost or worm castings.

Now, what you spend on the rest of the garden will really be as much or little as you want it to be. There are many cost-effective ways to build raised beds to your particular taste. For example, in our gardens, we repurposed old barnwood and galvanized roofing metal to build some beds, while a few of the others were laid directly into the ground, using the no-till method.

To create a garden that is truly unique and *yours*, you have to learn how to be resourceful. Of course, you can get yourself the fancy pieces, but nothing feels as rewarding as turning what others would think is useless into a functional work of art. We found some old cattle panels lying around the property and used them to make a grand arch that is now the centerpiece of our garden. Cattle panels overall have become a very inexpensive way for us to create arches and trellises all around the garden, along with cost-effective and eco-friendly bamboo.

We will dive even deeper into this topic in the next chapter, but if you really want to become self-sustaining, start your very own compost heap. That way, you're the one supplying your own garden with all the goodness it needs.

Even more economical techniques would be to start your plants from seed, save seeds from your garden, source from local farmers who are looking to get rid of organic material (straw, hay, manure, etc.) and catch your own rainwater (if legal in your area).

Creating the garden of your dreams, the payoff is invaluable. Nothing compares to eating a meal right from the garden, listening to the symphony of creatures who have made your garden their haven and sharing the joy of Mother Nature with the ones you love. To create a garden is one of the greatest investments you can make in yourself.

Of course, there is only so much we can think about prior to starting a garden. Life and Mother Nature will throw many unique challenges your way, but hopefully with some of the foresight provided here, you can better equip yourself with the knowledge I wish I had when I first started.

A vining Tromboncino squash supported by a repurposed cattle panel arch trellis. Getting creative in the garden can breathe new life into a variety of materials to maximize the effectiveness of your space.

No-Till Gardening

Why No-Till Gardening?

I need you to know that when I started my first garden, I did absolutely no research. My partner took the reins and I followed. He was used to the more conventional method of preparing the land for planting that is known as tilling the soil. Tilling is the act of digging 6 to 10 inches (5 to 20 cm) into the Earth to turn over and loosen the soil for easier planting, managing weeds and displacing pests. Without the proper equipment, it can be quite a grueling process. If you've ever worked with soil, you'd know it's heavy. So,

imagine having to dig up the Earth to turn it over and over and over again while also fighting deeply latched in roots, rocks and whatever else may be lurking below.

For my partner, this method was no problem. He was born to work with the Earth. He grew up exploring forests, splashing through swamps and collecting boulders (not rocks, boulders). His strength is fierce, and his will, unbreakable. To him, tilling the soil to prepare a garden bed was nothing. But for me, a frail city boy who couldn't even remember the last time he even felt dirt in his hands, this was a real challenge. Three turns in and I turned to him, out of breath and with pained disbelief in my eyes. "You can't be serious. There has to be another way."

I wanted a garden more than anything, and I knew there wasn't just an easier way, but a more harmonious way, to do this. As we tilled, I noticed we weren't just uprooting plants. Worms were getting caught up in the chaos, scrambling to find shelter after we ripped them from the safety of their burrows. I may not have known much about gardening at the time, but I knew worms were very important for the Earth. So, why were we disturbing them so much? It felt off.

That night, I literally sat down and Googled "painless ways to start a garden," and one of the first things to pop up was "no-till gardening." That simple Google search changed my life. You mean to tell me there was a way to start a garden without breaking my back? And people were still out here tilling? I was flabbergasted.

The further I dived into no-till gardening, the more confused I became. Why is this method not the standard? No-till is not just about saving you from the strain of relentlessly turning over dirt, it's about cultivating healthy soil as harmoniously as possible with Mother Nature.

I was worried about the worms, but the truth is, there is an entire WORLD of life right underneath our feet. You see, every thriving ecosystem on Earth depends on a vast network of life forms, including bacteria, fungi, worms and insects, which all call the soil their home. Each and every one of these organisms plays a significant role within the soil so that everything above can thrive. This delicately balanced ecosystem is something that Mother Nature has curated perfectly through generations upon generations of evolution. Why have we been disturbing something so precious? Especially when trying to start a garden? It's so backward. The foundation for abundance is already there. We just have to invigorate it.

When we till the soil, we completely uproot that ecosystem underneath the soil; we disrupt the network of life underneath the soil that can take many years to reestablish to the glory that it once was. The precious balance within the soil gets completely thrown out of whack when we turn it over into the harsh rays of the sun, scorching the delicate organisms that depend on the cool depths of the Earth to survive.

The soil beneath our feet is also one of the greatest resources we have in combating climate change. Every single plant that grows depends on carbon dioxide (CO_2) to thrive, absorbing it from the air and storing it within the soil underneath. When we till, all that carbon is released back into the air, dramatically increasing CO_2 emissions.

To ensure the preservation of the invaluable network of life beneath the soil, we can apply the no-till gardening method. The health of your soil is the most important instrument when orchestrating a healthy garden, not just for you, but in harmony with Mother Nature as well. If we want abundance above the soil, we must protect the abundance below.

The No-Till Garden Method Walkthrough

So, what exactly is no-till? It's curating a growing space while avoiding extreme disturbance of the soil. Yes! There is a way to create space for a garden without the strenuous, backbreaking labor of tilling. With no-till gardening, we're actually going to nourish the soil with minimal toil or disruption and really set ourselves up for an amazing growing season of abundance.

Before diving in, here is a list of essential tools and materials you'll need to get this going:

- A broad fork or pitchfork

- A pair of thick garden gloves and boots

- Biodegradable weed barrier, such as used cardboard or newspaper (a fair amount of it, enough to lay a ¼-inch (6-mm)-thick layer around the complete surface area of your bed)

- A hefty amount of garden soil, compost and/or worm castings. Enough to add a 3- to 5-inch (7.5- to 12.5-cm) layer of soil.

- A watering source

- A wheelbarrow (optional, but so helpful)

- Mulch—enough to spread a 2- to 3-inch (5- to 7.5-cm)-thick layer on the complete surface area of your bed. This should be undyed wood chips or organic straw/hay, depending on the intentions of your garden bed.

Step 1: Map Out Your Bed

To get started with the no-till gardening method, you first have to determine where you will be growing, how large you want your garden bed to be and what shape you want it to take. If you've gone ahead and created your garden plan, this is the perfect time to use it. Many naturalistic gardeners like to use circular shapes in their space to emulate the organic forms found in nature. If you're going for a more organized approach, you can section things off into more quadratic shapes, either directly in the ground or with raised beds. One of the many benefits of no-till gardening is the versatility of forms it can take.

For this walkthrough, I'll be using an in-ground rectangular plot as an example. It's important to note that you can apply this method on any type of ground that you're working with—a dry patch, a patch overrun with wild plants, a patch with rocky soil, sandy soil, and so on. It'll be effective no matter where you start. The purpose of this method is to bring life into the space you're working in. If you're working in a grassy area, it'll be really beneficial to mow and cut back the area you're working in. It'll be easier to prepare, and all the grass clippings will actually feed so much life back into the soil.

1

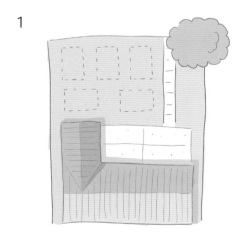

Step 2: Aerate the Soil

Now, using a broad fork or pitchfork, the first step to preparing a space for growing is aerating the soil, meaning we're going to slightly loosen the Earth and allow oxygen to flow through the cracks and reinvigorate all the organisms below the surface. This process is far less harmful to them than completely turning the soil and exposing them to the harsh rays of the sun. When aerating the soil, you want to make sure you get at least 8 inches (20 cm) into the ground to get a good amount of soil to lift up. Once you're in, you're gently going to push down on the end of your fork and slowly lift the Earth until cracks start to appear on the surface. Give it a few good nudges, then gently pull the fork out. Again, you do not want to flip the soil, just loosen it up a bit.

You'll start to get the hang of it after a few tries and you'll find your own rhythm. Once you get into the flow of it, go ahead and aerate the soil in the complete area that you're preparing for growing. This is the most strenuous part of the no-till method, but it's minuscule in effort compared to tilling. Your back will thank you.

2

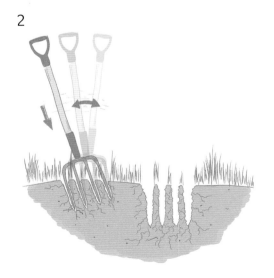

I do want to note that, when aerating the soil, this would be a great time to really examine the space you're working in for really mature wild perennial plants that have established large root systems. While the biodegradable weed barrier will help manage most annual plants and shorter rooted plants, it'll take a little extra work to take care of those really old established roots. If you stumble upon any while aerating, it is best to uproot the main rhizome, or the central subterranean-nean stem that produces shoots and roots, or else it'll keep sending out runners in the future. It pains me to have to disturb the soil so much if I find a very old root, but it'll be really difficult to kill off with a weed barrier alone and it'll hinder your garden bed from thriving later on.

Once you've completely aerated the soil, give it a light watering to moisten. This will help the breaking-down process of biomaterials.

Step 3: Lay Down Weed Barrier

Next, we can add our layer of biodegradable weed barrier. Used cardboard is my preferred material. It's thick and lays on very easily, depending on the size of the cardboard. If using cardboard, make sure you're using something with little ink and avoid anything that's heavily printed on or glossy. Newspaper works just as well, but you'll have to get enough of it to apply a very thick layer over the area you're prepping. Don't worry about the ink on the newspapers, as most of their inks are water- or soy-based.

Adding this layer of weed barrier is essential, especially if you're working in an area that was previously overgrown. The purpose of the weed barrier is to block out the light so as to kill off any existing plants. It's important to clear the space of existing plants, other-wise they will compete with everything you plan on growing yourself and hinder the success of your garden. What's so incredibly fascinating about this process is that, as the plants die off, they slowly break down (with the help of our organisms beneath the ground) and feed life back into the soil. This will give the Earth an incredible boost, and your future plants will have a plethora of nutrients at their disposal.

What's even more fascinating is that carbon-based materials, such as cardboard and paper, attract a variety of desirable organisms under the soil—most importantly, worms. Worms are the superstars of the soil. They eat a wide array of biomaterials and leave their nutrient-rich worm castings in their place, while also tunneling through the Earth, creating a network of airways that help oxygenate and loosen the soil.

It can take a few months for the cardboard and newspaper to fully break down, but you don't have to wait for it to fully decompose to start planting. Once the area is prepared, I like to come back a few weeks after to lift up a sheet of cardboard and see how many worms it has attracted. It's exciting to see how effective the cardboard is at luring them in. I'm always so amazed to see the dozens upon dozens of slimy friends that felt invited into my space thanks to the cardboard. The more native worms you have in your garden, the better!

Step 4: Soak the Weed Barrier

To help your weed barrier break down more quickly, you're going to need to give it a heavy soak. You want to really saturate the material before moving on to the next step. So, grab a hose or watering can and drench it!

3

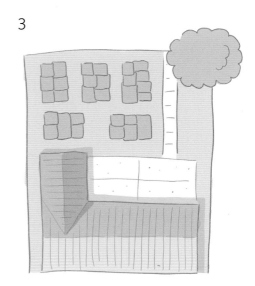

4

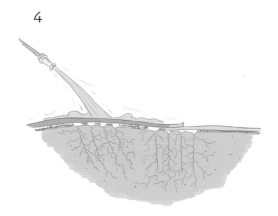

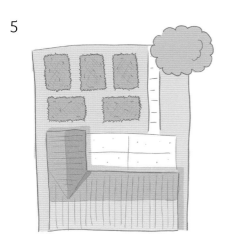

5

Step 5: Lay Down Your Soil

Once your weed barrier is nice and damp, you can start adding your garden soil, compost and/or worm castings. I personally love to use a nice 3- to 5-inch (7.5- to 12.5-cm) layer of 50:50 compost and worm castings, because it adds an incredible blend of nutrients and overall goodness for the soil. Both can be sourced from a local garden or horticultural center. It's best to buy in bulk to save you some money. This is where the wheelbarrow would really come in handy. It's a lot easier wheeling larger loads than carrying individual bags.

Step 6: Lay Down Mulch

The final step in preparing your bed is spreading it with a nice layer of mulch. Mulch is so important! When you add fresh garden soil, compost or worm castings, you're also adding even more organisms already living within the medium. This new network of life you're introducing to your soil is precious and will add to the already existing ecosystem. We want to make sure they are protected so they can thrive in their new home. As noted earlier, these organisms are incredibly sensitive to the UV rays of the sun and can actually die if directly exposed for too long. Adding that layer of mulch will protect them from these rays while also providing more food as it breaks down over time.

The type of mulch you use is really dependent on what you're intending to grow in your new bed. For ornamental beds more focused on flowers, shrubs or trees, its best to use a wood chip mulch. For fruits and veggies, opt for straw (the by-product of harvests, typically free of seeds that would otherwise cause weeds to arise). Wood mulches leach acidity into the soil that most fruits and veggies don't really like, so opting for straw is always best for them. Hay is used for feed and isn't so processed, meaning it'll

most likely carry more seeds. Try your best to get organic straw. You never want to use anything that has been sprayed with pesticides, because it'll eventually leach into the soil and negatively impact the ecosystem you're trying so hard to cultivate.

Another benefit to adding a layer of mulch is that it's going to help retain moisture in your beds for longer, because your soil is not directly exposed to the hot and drying rays of the sun. It'll speed up the breakdown process of biomaterials and you'll have to water your garden less often.

Make sure you add a nice 2- to 3-inch (5- to 7.5-cm) layer of mulch, or enough to completely cover the soil. You don't want to see any of your dirt peeking through the straw.

Step 7: Planting in a No-Till Bed

Technically, you can start to plant right away. When planting into a brand-new bed, I like to use sharp-edged tools to cut completely through the cardboard layer into the areas I'm sowing seeds or transplanting seedlings into. Then, I remove the cardboard to expose the space where my plant will be growing. Before planting, I also work the soil within the hole to loosen it up for easy root growth. The newly laid cardboard or newspaper can be a bit challenging for growing roots to navigate through, so it helps clear the way for them.

It's important to note that if you plant directly into a freshly prepared bed, it may take a bit longer for new plants to establish, as they may have to compete with the dying root systems of the covered plants below.

I've immediately planted into newly prepared beds with great results, but I've noticed a difference when planting into beds that I've let undergo the full breaking-down process. If you want your bed to undergo the breaking-down process first, it's best to start in the fall so that it's ready to go in the spring. Or if you don't want to get the entire bed ready just yet, you can lay a tarp down in the area you want to prepare in the fall, to kill off any existing plants, so that it's further along in the process for a new bed in the spring.

Once I tried no-till gardening, I never went back. It's the only way I garden now. It's incredibly simple, requires far less labor and it's versatile. You can use the no-till method to prepare garden beds directly in the soil or even as your foundation for raised beds. All you have to do is dig your raised beds in first, then continue with no-till.

7

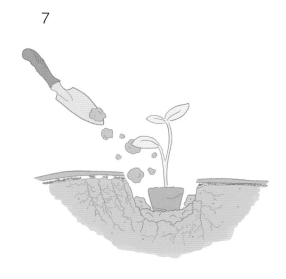

Growing in Raised Beds

The beauty of no-till gardening is how versatile it can be. It can even be used to prepare a space for raised beds, rather than overworking the soil and breaking your back in the process. Raised beds are an incredible way to create a home for plants, even if you don't have the best soil in your growing space. Raised beds allow you to create a growing space separate from the existing soil by adding your own special mix of amendments. For example, if you're looking to grow but your soil is very sandy or too rocky to work in, building a raised bed is an ideal solution to avoid dealing with hard-to-grow-in soils. Being able to create your own growing environments gives you the opportunity to really tailor the conditions to the plants you're cultivating. When growing in raised beds, make sure you're using soil mix that retains more moisture, as raised beds have a tendency to dry more quickly because of their elevation and warmed edges. To help your beds retain moisture longer, add a 2- to 3-inch (5- to 7.5-cm) layer of mulch on top to prevent the sun's rays from drying the soil too quickly.

Many growers opt in for raised beds because they also create a barrier between weeds and the plants you're focused on growing. The defined edges of raised beds make it very easy to organize your growing space as well. A unique feature of raised beds is the height they can offer. They come in many different shapes, sizes and materials. For those who find it more difficult to crouch down to ground level, a high raised bed would be ideal. I've even seen raised beds on legs so they can be right at waist level.

To get the most out of your raised beds, I recommend investing in metal frames. It may be a bit more costly up front, but they can last for a very long time. If you want to use a wooden frame, I'd recommend pressure-treated wood or cedar. Both will last much longer than untreated lumber. I've seen people get really creative with cinder blocks as well, layering two of them to create the frame of the bed. Cinder blocks are strong and durable; depending on how you lay them, you can use their openings for smaller individual growing spaces.

Now, let's talk about actually installing a raised bed in the garden. Make sure you're completely aware of the space you have available and the exact measurements of the beds you're looking to put together. I would build the frame of your bed and lay it over the area where you plan to install it. Then, with a spade or a sharp-edged tool, carve the outline of the frame into the ground. Once you have your shape outlined, remove the frame from that area. With your spade, dig out a 6-inch (15-cm)-deep trench that is wide enough to fit the frame of your raised bed. The width will vary, depending on the bed. You want a nice depth for your bed to fit into, so it can remain tightly secured in place and prevent any running weeds from crawling underneath. Once you've dug out your trench, carefully maneuver your frame into it. Dig the edges of your bed in with the excess soil and firmly press the ground to lock the bed in place.

Lilium "Nettie's Pride," a favorite in the garden.

Once your bed is in place, you can apply the no-till gardening method (see page 55). Regardless of the height of the bed, if there is soil underneath, I recommend aerating the soil and placing that layer of biodegradable weed barrier to invigorate the microbes in the area. If you want a very controlled space, without the hassle of opportunistic plants reclaiming your growing space, lay cardboard or the weed barrier of your choosing down on the walkways between your beds and finish it off with a layer of wood mulch or gravel. This will prevent any weeds from growing in the walkways and it will be much easier to manage your garden. It's a functional design, easier to manage and aesthetically pleasing.

As mentioned before, raised beds can dry out rather quickly, so when it comes to managing your beds, make sure you're staying on top of watering. A great benefit to raised beds is being able to control all the contents within them, so you'll really be able to give your plants everything they need and more. Over time, the soil will deplete as it continues to break down and feed your plants. For the best results from your beds, take care that they are well filled with soil. You want only about a 1- to 2-inch (2.5- to 5-cm) gap between the soil and the top edge of your frame. At the start of each season, add new amendments, such as compost or raised bed garden mix, to replenish all that was broken down the year before.

Raised beds offer an accessibility to growing for many gardeners. Whether you're in a space with soil that's hard to grow in or a backyard that's completely concrete, you still have the opportunity to grow an immense abundance with the help and versatility of raised beds. At the end of the day, it's all about how determined you are to grow, and raised beds make it very possible.

Container Gardening

If you have limited space, are renting and don't want to commit to breaking ground or only have access to a balcony, you still have the potential to grow with the help of containers. Container gardening offers so much abundance and versatility. If you want to dip your toes into the world of gardening, starting with a container is the way to do it. What makes it even more fun is the wide array of containers you could use, and if you're really inspired, you can create your own! All you need to do is drill drainage holes at the bottom of anything you'd like to use to house your plants. Get creative; plants are resilient creatures. You'd be very surprised to see what plants can grow in.

Every house plant grower can understand the potential of growing in pots—it's limitless! Well, as long as you have the room for it. I have to warn you: Once you start, it's really hard to stop. I remember getting my very first *Monstera deliciosa* in my Brooklyn apartment and feeling the immediate urge to fill every inch of my space with plants. I just needed to make sure my plants had access to light, were well watered and were consistently spritzed to uphold their need for moisture on the leaves. When growing in containers, be sure to use a potting medium that retains moisture well but has good drainage. You don't want your plants sitting in water for too long, and you especially don't want them drying out for too long. The frequency of waterings will ultimately depend on the plant, its size and the size of the pot it's growing in. Also, if you want your plants to grow their large beautiful foliage, you need to make sure you're supplementing them with the necessary nutrients. Plants gotta eat! Be sure to get your plants on a consistent fertilizing schedule.

Many houseplants are actually endemic to areas with tropical climates and they can get very large if cared for effectively. At some point, houseplants will outgrow their pot and need to be repotted into something larger to be able to grow to their fullest potential. I highly suggest researching the conditions where the plants originate from, so that you can provide them with everything they need to thrive. Seeing the monsteras when I visited Costa Rica for the first time stopped me dead in my tracks. I could not believe how big they were! Seeing them in their natural habitat really helped me understand how they liked to grow. Seeing them sprawl up the trunks of enormous trees to find refuge from the sun under the canopy taught me how they love a lot of light, but not direct sunlight. It also taught me how they like to climb and that they need support. Feeling

the humidity on my skin made me realize just how much moisture they pull from the air. Walking on layers of decaying leaves on the forest floor showed me just how well fed they were. To really understand how a plant likes to live, visit them in their home. It's the best way to understand how to make your home theirs.

Besides growing houseplants, container gardening offers you the chance to grow your own food indoors or on your balcony! If you're growing indoors, the key to success is supplementing the light your plants will need to thrive by using grow lights. If you're growing on a balcony or patio, the types of plants you can grow will ultimately depend on the amount of light you get in your outdoor space. If you get at least six hours of direct sunlight, you can grow some heat-loving crops, such as tomatoes, peppers and eggplants. If your space gets more shade throughout the day, you could grow leafy greens, kale and carrots. It never hurts to experiment to learn just how much potential your growing space has. If the container is large enough, you could even interplant companion plants to get the most out of your pots. No matter your circumstance, the potential is there. All you need to do is try.

Chapter 6

A Deeper Understanding of Soil Health

The World Beneath Our Feet

Gardens are more than meets the eye. When we gaze upon a luscious green space, we're enamored by the rich abundance of plants swaying in the wind, dazzling us with a vibrant display of color and texture. But the true magic of any naturescape actually happens beyond the limits of our sight. Beneath the surface lies a bustling network of microscopic life that is responsible for all the wonders that happen above. You see, soil is *alive*.

But what exactly is soil? Within the boundary between the Earth's inanimate rock and luscious green carpet lies a delicious brew of minerals, organic matter, liquids and even gases. The contents of this earthy cocktail varies from region to region, but the most fascinating role of these soils is their potential to house life. The richer the diversity of organic matter that is present within the soil, the richer the diversity of bacteria, fungi, insects and worms that can call this place home. To give you a glimpse of just how abundant in numbers these little creatures are, a single teaspoon of established garden soil may contain billions of these tiny organisms.

This immense network of organisms is integral to the success of not just our gardens, but every ecosystem around the world. To better care for our gardens, we must look at what nature has perfected already.

Soil is where the deceased are given new life. We know that every living thing must one day meet its end, but nature teaches us that death is just as natural a part of life as living. This is where soil organisms come in. They take what is left behind and recycle it into a nutrient-rich source of life for the world above. With enough goodness in the soil, these organisms can harbor almost all of the nutrients that plants need.

When we think of our gardens, we must understand what is really orchestrating before us. As we feed the soil and introduce a diversity of plants, we are becoming the composers of an ecosystem. These ecosystems are a hierarchy with tiers that are dependent on the success of the tier below them. But none of them will ever thrive without a strong foundation of a diverse network of life in the soil. The greater the diversity of life in the soil, the greater the diversity of life above. *Life brings life.*

Without this integral structure of life within the Earth, all life as we know it would collapse. In a well-aged ecosystem, all the creatures within its web have developed a dependence on one another through many years of evolution. Studies have shown that certain plants can thrive only if certain organisms are present within the soil. These bacteria and fungi are the tether between plants and the Earth, and if anything were to happen to them, the chain could be severed. The population of the dependent plants would dwindle, meaning the population of the insects that depend on those plants would dwindle, meaning the population of the small mammals that depend on those insects would dwindle, meaning the population of the predatory birds that depends on those small mammals would dwindle, and so on. The balance within ancient ecosystems has taken nature millions of years to build, yet all it takes is the absence of a single organism to throw the balance off kilter. These sacred spaces are fragile. That is why it's imperative that we learn how to care for them from the ground up.

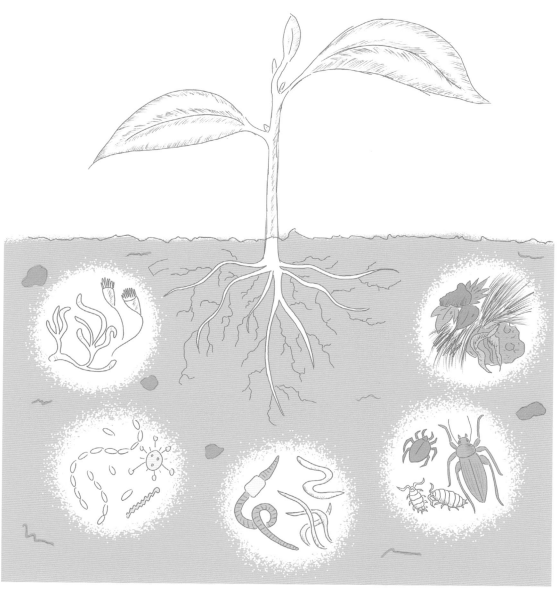

A diagram of the many forms of life beneath the soil. From left to right you have fungi, bacteria, worms, decomposers and decaying biomatter.

Preserving the Underworld

The abundance that we see in the natural world is a reflection of the abundance below. A thriving and biodiverse ecosystem is nothing without the richness of life underneath. That is why it is essential that we preserve the precious ecology that already exists. The purpose of a garden should not be to disrupt, but to harmonize, encourage and restore.

Tragically, humans have done a masterful job of depleting the soils of our land through excessive and aggressive agricultural practices that involve pillaging hectares of earth for barren monocultures of crops. The systems in place are designed to produce an overabundance of a single crop at the cost of completely disrupting the rich balance of life that once was. On top of that, the excessive use of pesticides, herbicides and fertilizers has left these landscapes completely devoid of life.

In our gardens, we have the chance to change that. Rather than tilling the soil and using chemicals, we can sculpt our dream spaces in the ways Mother Nature has designed. It's imperative that we look at and study her ways and implement them in our own practices so that we can grow the healthiest abundance possible while harmonizing with the natural world around us. It is possible. It can be done. And it starts with preserving the health of our soil, or better yet, feeding life into it.

When creating a garden bed, I highly recommend applying the no-till garden method; it's a great way of preserving the ecology and structure of your soil without the aggressive and back-breaking disruption of tilling or turning the soil. I've given you a full walk-through in the previous chapter.

Feeding Life into the Soil

Through careful observation of well-established wild ecosystems, we've come to develop a few different methods of feeding the soils of our gardens. These practices are creating and using compost, mulching and planting cover crops.

Composting

If you've gardened, you've heard about compost, but what exactly is it? In simple terms, compost is the nutrient-rich soil-like by-product of decomposed organic matter. To create a delicious blend of compost, it must be well balanced between carbon and nitrogen. Carbon-rich materials are such things as wood chips, paper, cardboard, pine shavings, straw, hay and sawdust. Nitrogen-rich materials are such things as manure, grass clippings, freshly fallen leaves, garden or plant-based kitchen scraps, bone meal and fish scraps. Avoid bones, meat, fats and oils, as they will take too long to break down and attract unwanted critters. When we are creating compost, we're essentially creating an environment for microbes to thrive so

that they can break down the organic matter to make our nutrient-rich material. For the microbes to perform their best, they need a balanced carbon-to-nitrogen ratio of 30:1. Simply put, you'll need far more carbon-rich organic matter than nitrogen.

A few key factors of a healthy compost are size, temperature and moisture. To ensure your heap or bin of compost can insulate well enough, you want to build it up to at least 3 feet (about 90 cm). Something fascinating happens when you have a large, well-balanced heap of compost. It starts to *cook*. That means the microbes are hard at work, breaking everything down. Ideally, a good range of temperature for successfully breaking down your compost is between 120 and 150°F (50 and 66°C). There are special compost thermometers you can use to test your temperatures.

Moisture is also essential for a compost heap to thrive. The microbes prefer an environment that is warm and moist, so when I'm adding my materials, I'm sure to shower them with water in the process. You don't want it to be soggy, but as moist as a wrung-out sponge or paper towel.

Something I personally like to do to add a richness of life to my compost is to also mix in a few spadefuls of already broken-down compost to help give it a boost. It can be very helpful to outsource your materials from local farms, canneries, lumber companies, produce warehouses or even fallen leaves from your yard or even the forest (sustainably, of course—don't take more than you need).

If your compost is well balanced, it can take anywhere from six to nine months to fully break down. There are times when a compost heap can go stale, meaning it stops cooking. To reinvigorate your compost, you can simply flip it to reintroduce oxygen to the microbes or throw in some fresh nitrogen-rich materials, such as grass clippings.

Once your compost is broken down well enough, you can use it to feed your soil by spreading a 2- to 3-inch (5- to 7.5-cm) layer on your beds at the beginning of the growing season. There is nothing more rewarding than sustainably creating your own source of goodness for your gardens. Creating enough organic matter to feed your gardens can be quite challenging, especially if you have larger or multiple gardens to feed. Luckily, compost that has already been prepared is easy to source from local garden or horticulture centers. To be more cost effective, I'd recommend buying in bulk by the yard rather than in individual bags. If you end up with a surplus of compost, it never hurts to add an abundance of compost to your beds, or you could add it to your existing compost heap.

THREE-BIN COMPOSTING

Three-bin composting is a composting technique that involves using three separate bins to create a continuous cycle of compost production. The idea is to have one bin for new materials, one for actively decomposing materials and one for finished compost.

The first bin is where you add fresh organic material, such as food scraps, yard waste and other compostable items. This bin is where the composting process begins, as the materials will begin to decompose over time.

Once the first bin is full, you'll start filling the second bin with fresh material while allowing the first bin to decompose. You'll want to regularly turn and mix the materials in the bins to promote the breakdown of the organic matter. Every four to six weeks, I use a pitchfork to toss around the piles, to keep the compost active.

As the materials in the second bin decompose, you'll eventually have finished compost that can be used in your garden or for other purposes, which can then be moved over to the third bin. Once moved, you'll have an empty bin to begin the process again.

By having three separate bins, you can create a continuous cycle of compost production. This method ensures that you always have fresh compost available and minimizes the time it takes to produce high-quality homemade compost.

CHICKENS AND THE GARDEN

Raising chickens is such a fulfilling experience. They are endless entertainment with their unwavering curiosity and antics. They provide an abundance of eggs, a rich source of protein, and they're of great benefit to your garden!

We keep the chicken coop right next to the vegetable garden and our compost. For bedding in the coop, the area where the chickens lay and roost, we use pine shavings. One thing about chickens is that they're messy and they poop. A lot. But that's great for the garden! Every two to three weeks in the warmer months, their bedding is cleaned out and replaced. I'll be honest—it's my least favorite chore. It's hot, stuffy and stinks. Not to mention, there are projectile poops that have hardened on the walls and need to be scraped off. It's nasty, hard work. But the powerful role the bedding plays in the garden is so worth it. When the bedding is removed from the coop, it goes straight to the compost. The pine shavings and chicken manure are an incredible mix of brown and green biomaterial that is jam-packed with nitrogen and other important minerals. In fact, chicken manure is so powerful that it needs to break down for a few months before adding it to the garden or it can literally burn your plants from the overwhelming abundance of nutrients. To give our compost even more of a boost, we throw in our eggshells as well. These are a great source of calcium, an important nutrient that strengthens plants. I crush them up before tossing them in, to speed up the breaking-down process.

During the colder months, I apply the *deep bedding* method in the coop, continuously adding a layer of pine shavings every month rather than swapping it out. Through the winter, the bedding builds up and helps keep the coop warm. In the spring, I do a massive cleaning of the coop and throw three to four months' worth of bedding into the compost, completely restoring all the broken-down compost that I used to replenish the garden beds.

Mulch Magic

Another incredible way to not only build life within your soil but to protect it is by laying down *mulch*. Mulch is organic material, such as wood chips or straw, which is used to cover a bed. There are numerous benefits to laying down mulch as it pertains to soil health.

First, over time, organic mulches break down and become a source of food for the ecosystem of organisms below. Something to be conscious of is that different types of mulch bring different influences to your garden bed. For example, wood mulches or pine shavings are higher in acidity than straw or hay so, over time, they'll slowly elevate the acidity in your soil. For ornamental gardens, this can pose no threat, but for vegetables, this can affect their growth. That is why it is usually suggested to use organic straw or hay to mulch vegetable beds, as they leach far less acidity into the soil.

Besides becoming food over time, mulch protects your underground organisms from the intense UV light that could easily kill them. The delicate network of life below prefers a moist and cooler climate. Mulch keeps your soil cooler and stops its moisture from evaporating too quickly. This will also save you from watering nearly as much throughout the season.

To get the most out of your mulch, it's recommended to place a 2- to 4-inch (5- to 10-cm) layer over your beds. The timing in which you lay your mulch is up to you. Personally, I like to lay my mulch once my bed is prepared for the season and before planting. It's easier for me to spread the mulch thickly and quickly without any plants in the way. When it comes time for planting, I simply brush the mulch away from the area I'm planting in and reapply it when I'm done.

Cover Crops

The final practice that has proven to be incredibly impactful in the garden is the use of *cover crops*. For more immediate preparations of spaces for planting, I'd recommend using compost and mulch, but if you're looking to prepare a larger space for long-term fertility and planting, cover crops are an excellent resource. Cover crops are specific plants utilized in spaces for their unique properties that influence the nutrients within the soil or its structure, or to smother large groupings of weeds.

The use and maintenance of cover crops varies from plant to plant, but they can be a valuable resource depending on your needs. If you have soil that is deprived of nutrients,

there are cover crops you can plant to replenish it, such as nitrogen-fixing clover or legumes. Something to note when using cover crops to feed your soils: Be sure to cut or mow them back before they flower, unless you want them to reseed. The decision is yours.

If you have soil that needs loosening and aerating, rapeseed, mustard or even radishes can help open it up. Another amazing use for cover crops is to attract beneficial pollinators, such as by planting buckwheat, clovers and vetch. Even more fascinating, some cover crops have intersectional roles, meaning you can get multiple benefits from them.

Comfrey

While on the topic of beneficial plants for the health of your soil, I cannot pass up the opportunity to talk about one of my favorite plants in the garden that has offered endless abundance: *comfrey.*

Comfrey is a perennial plant that has been used for generations for its amazing medicinal properties, but it can play a significant role in feeding your gardens as well. You see, comfrey grows a very large and very deep taproot that is able to access nutrients that many other plants cannot. It pulls up these nutrients, making its leaves rich with goodness.

I personally like to let my comfrey go to flower before harvesting the leaves. Pollinators just love them. But once their flowering cycle is complete, I grab my scythe and harvest the leaves to use in a variety of ways. To be more specific, comfrey swells up a richness of potassium in its leaves, which is an essential nutrient for fruiting plants, such as tomatoes, peppers and squashes. To get the most out of my comfrey, I use it in three ways.

My favorite way to use it is by making a comfrey tea fertilizer. To do so, I simply gather enough leaves to fill a 5-gallon (19-L) bucket halfway. Then, I fill the rest of the bucket with water and cover it with a lid once it reaches the top. I set the bucket aside for two weeks and let the leaves "brew." After two weeks, I lift the lid and brace myself, because the stench is absolutely horrid. But that's how I know it worked. I scoop out the remaining biomaterial and toss it into the compost. What I'm left with is a nutrient-rich cocktail. I then pour the tea into gallon (3.8-L)-sized containers to store it. When using it to feed my plants, I fill a watering pitcher about one-tenth of the way with my tea and fill the

rest with rainwater to dilute it. It's powerful stuff. I stay on a biweekly schedule of feeding my plants and I'm sure to water them directly into their roots. The abundance throughout the growing season says it all: They love it.

The second way to use comfrey is to simply bury the leaves in the garden beds next to your plants. They will act as a slow-release fertilizer, gently adding nutrients to the soil as they break down.

Third, if I harvest an overabundance of comfrey, I throw what remains into my compost heap, to give it an amazing nutrient-rich boost.

A few things to note with comfrey. It can grow very vigorously, so be sure to plant it in a space where it will have room to grow. It thrives in full sun to part shade. And again, it is perennial, so if it's happy, it will come back for you year after year. Also, the leaves and stems of comfrey have very small spines, so be sure to wear long sleeves, full-length pants and gloves when working with it.

I truly hope this chapter illuminates the importance of soil and conserving the precious ecosystem living within it. Mother Earth offers immense abundance, and we as her inhabitants have a responsibility to preserve its wonders. Unfortunately, humanity has paved a path of overconsumption and recklessness that has placed immense pressure on the delicate balance she has spent millions of years creating. But it doesn't have to be this way. For our tremendous ability to destroy, we have an even greater ability to create. If we pay close attention and follow in the footsteps of Mother Nature, we won't just peacefully coexist, we will all thrive in pure abundance. And it begins in the soil.

The luscious leaves of a comfrey plant.>

Chapter 7

Saving Our Soils

Understanding births empathy. When we learn about the world of life beneath our feet, we forge a bond with it. Without that precious civilization under the Earth, nothing would grow. That is why it's so important that we not only learn to cultivate it, we must fight to protect it. The way humans have industrialized our planet has left it scarred and hurting. To understand the way we can save what remains and rebuild what was lost, we must learn the history of our relationship with Earth. Only then can we stop history from repeating.

When you work in the garden, there's this synchronicity that happens between you and the environment around you. You come to understand the way things should be. Working with the soil, tending to the plants and interacting with all the creatures in between deeply attunes you to the rhythm of nature. I've learned to respect the land we are on because it holds the life that provides for us. *When we care for the land, the land cares for us.*

In my journey to learn how to grow food, I became curious about large-scale farming operations and how they went about growing their crops. I pulled up my chair and opened my laptop. My fingers tapped across the keyboard: "How is food grown in America?"

My eyes widened. "Industrialization." "Pesticides." "Destruction."

I mean, I knew the system wasn't the greatest, but I didn't realize it was downright corrupt. There were countless articles discussing dying soils, unhealthy produce and the industry's sole priority being profits. One story led me to the documentary *Kiss the Ground* on Netflix. I took a deep breath and started watching.

When the ending credits started, I had tears in my eyes. I was both extremely grateful and disgusted. Grateful for being able to grow my own food, knowing it's safe and grown with the utmost care. Disgusted by the trauma modern agriculture has inflicted on our planet and our people. This system isn't just harming the environment; it's making us sick.

Mother Nature has perfected her system for providing abundance and it all begins in the soil. Without healthy soil, we have nothing. You'd think this simple understanding would be a core principle when working with land to grow our sustenance. Wrong. So gut wrenchingly wrong.

The development of large-scale agriculture has become one of the most destructive systems the planet has ever witnessed. The impacts of decimating approximately five billion hectares, more than one-third of once thriving lands, is being felt across the globe. You see, the health of our planet is directly linked to the health of our climate. Thick forests full of shading trees cooled the ground below. They cycled moisture from the soil through the pores of their leaves out into the atmosphere, causing enough humidity to build up to bring forth rain. The abundance of plants would also breathe in gigatons of carbon dioxide, pull it down their shoots to their roots and feed it to the network of soil microbes below. The carbon that microbes didn't need was released back into the Earth, where it was stored. This cycle has been repeating for millions of years.

In modern farming, a vicious cycle of clearing land, tilling the soil and pumping it with chemicals has taken hold.

In industrial agriculture, land is prepared for growing massive monocultures of a single crop. To do so, they uproot and chop down every plant in sight because those are seen as competition to their cash crops. Afterward, they till these clear-cuts to loosen the soil and kill off any surviving root systems. Hectares of bustling landscapes were decimated. Once the unnaturally large groupings of crops were planted, other plants, pests, fungi and even nutrients are strictly controlled through dense applications of herbicides, pesticides, fungicides and synthetic fertilizers. These chemicals may provide quick results, but the cesspool of toxins kills off every remaining sign of life beneath the Earth.

After nearly a century of this loop, the soil of these plundered lands has died. All of this feels so backward. These horrendous practices go against everything Mother Nature has taught us. She already provides us with so much abundance. How could we treat our planet this way? How could our system be so inhumane? How did we get here?

I wish I never asked. I'm going to need you to sit down for this.

The story of our modern agriculture system begins during World War II. In a time where food was scarce, German scientist Fritz Haber invented a process for creating synthetic nitrogen fertilizer. He continued on to craft the poisons used to create the first chemical weapons in our history. The impact this had on the battlefield was cataclysmic. Once the war was over, U.S. chemical companies hauled these poisons home with plans of mass-producing them. The end of the war left America with an immense surplus of resources. Can you guess where they redirected these resources?

Farms. The end of World War II birthed the largest industrial food production operation the world had ever seen. The chemical companies produced their toxic synthetics, branded them as pesticides and sold them to farms across the country. The campaign was such a roaring success that the use of pesticides became an integral part of the agricultural system we have today.

Overtilling and overwhelming plantings of singular crops do irreversible damage to the soil. Farmers are now trapped in a vicious cycle of using pesticides and synthetic fertilizers because the soil won't provide on its own. It's barren. And many can't afford to go a season without producing any crops. Now, most if not all crops grown in these operations have been genetically modified to withstand the toxicity of these chemicals. The excessive use of these chemicals over the past few decades has caused them to leach into our food and waters.

I'm sorry to say that it doesn't end there. The devastating impact to the environment isn't the only symptom of the industrial agriculture machine. Remember when I mentioned carbon getting stored in the soil? Tilling causes the carbon to erupt from the reservoir below and the web of life responsible for filtering that carbon back into the Earth is gone. With nothing to sequester it, the carbon continues to build in the atmosphere. This tremendous buildup of carbon dioxide is what traps heat and warms our planet. Modern-day agriculture is one of the largest contributors to CO_2 emissions and has left one-third of the world's land infertile. But here's the thing. It doesn't have to be this way.

The agricultural systems in place are not designed to care for the soil. They are strictly designed to mass-produce no matter the environmental cost. When we observe the ways of nature, we see it has the phenomenal ability to restore itself. It regenerates. Everything that dies is reborn. This focus on regeneration has fabricated a method of growing tremendous amounts of food while invigorating the land that it's being grown on. Harmony.

Regenerative Farming

We already know that soil has the incredible ability to house and create life, but it can also hold more carbon than plants and the atmosphere, combined. And what's even more fascinating, is that if the conditions are right, the soil can capture that carbon very quickly. Through the practice of *regenerative farming*, we can create the perfect conditions for that to happen.

In the simplest of terms, all regenerative farming is doing is restoring the soil through the reintroduction of a diverse range of plants, soil organisms and creatures. It allows us to grow food at its maximum potential, producing more food per acre than traditional farming. Rather than growing a monoculture of plants, we can grow *food forests*. To revive a piece of land, we have to start by rebuilding the topsoil. Without tilling, the soil is able to store more water, which increases the amount of microbes, which increases the amount of plants that can thrive there, which increases humidity, which allows for more rainfall, thus reestablishing the cycle of water to the environment. To further reinvigorate the soil, we can introduce plants, such as cover crops, that can grow well in poorer

soils while also filtering back in carbon and other nutrients. A wide range of plants in a space means a large range of plant exudates feeding the soil, which only further increases the diversity of small organisms. If livestock is introduced, the potential for restoration is even greater. Livestock grazes on the abundance of cover crops and feeds the soil with their manure, increasing the amount of microbes even more. At this point, an ecosystem has been established and the land cares for itself, growing more and more abundant each year. The data show us that regenerative farming, practiced on a global level, can single-handedly tip the scales of carbon emissions. Rather than decimating land and filling our atmosphere with more carbon, we can rebirth entire ecosystems and sequester carbon. It is possible and it is being done.

I had the incredible privilege of visiting a regenerative dairy farm in the luscious rolling green hills of Vermont. Seeing the amount of love and care that went into this farm's operation left me full of hope. I witnessed firsthand how this farm was feeding a diversity of life back into the soil through cover

crops. The farm also controlled where its livestock grazes throughout the year, to allow the natural cycle of the plants to play out. What was once barren farmland was now a thriving ecosystem that was storing tons of carbon in the process.

This is where I learned the difference between *dirt* and *soil*. Dirt is devoid of life, passing through my fingertips as I pick it up to get a closer look. Soil is *rich, moist* and *alive*. One of the farm ecologists had us probe the soil and feel it in our hands, but what struck me the most wasn't the sensation of the cool soil in my hands. It was the smell. I closed my eyes and brought the sample closer to my nose. The cool, damp scent filled my nostrils. It quite literally grounded me.

If we take action to completely reshape the way we grow food on our planet on a global level, then we'll have the opportunity to *cool the planet*. The same practices that will heal our soil will also heal our climate.

Now, you may be wondering why I am telling you this. You see, the practices of conventional farming have trickled down and influenced home-scale gardening. We go to the garden center or farm co-op and we still see these toxic chemicals marketed to us. The use of these materials is still a very common practice to help vanquish weeds and manage pests. But what we've seen through the miracle of regenerative farming is that it doesn't have to be this way. We can take the philosophies of regeneration and apply them in our own gardens. We can create our very own thriving ecosystems right in our backyards. Our gardens should be a place of restoration, harmony and abundance.

Above all, regenerative gardening of all scales plays its part in sequestering carbon and reversing the effects of climate change. If we apply these practices in our backyards, it can ripple through our communities and inspire those around us to lead a more naturally connected practice in their gardens and life. If you aren't able to grow your own food just yet, I urge you to support farms that are aligned with regenerative philosophies. At the end of the day, the greatest influence we have as the consumers is where we spend our money. If we put the power back into our own hands and into the hands of the farmers, we can reshape the way we grow food and help heal the planet in the process. I want future generations to experience the abundance we've created through our choices. It is possible. It can be done.

< *Hand feeding a dairy cow from an organic dairy farm.*

Chapter 8
Building Biodiversity

Building biodiversity is the best way to manage your gardens while also encouraging a thriving community of native wildlife. In this chapter, I dive in and give you more insight on ways you can continue to build biodiversity in your gardens.

Planting Native Plants

In our gardens, we have a special opportunity to compose a harmonious symphony of plants. Not just plants that we can benefit from, but wildlife as well. We can create a beautiful flow of energies between Nature's creatures, the plants we introduce and the soil that we tend. Think of each plant as an instrument, playing its own melody, bringing forth its own community of players. These players are your local native wildlife that can benefit your garden if invited to perform.

To invite them, all we need to do is plant native species of plants that will provide shelter and food. These new homes play into the ecology of your garden and help it take care of itself. For example, I've planted a wide variety of native trees, shrubs and flowering plants at the far edge of my garden. And guess what? When you plant native, you're helping native wildlife and you reap the benefits. The trees and shrubs invite birds and small mammals to rest and feed on the berries and bugs. In return, they help maintain bug populations in the garden while also fertilizing the soil with their droppings. Trees and shrubs also help sustain the ecology of the soil. When it rains, the droplets cleanse their leaves and become filled with nutrients as they make their descent to the soil, providing suste-

nance for the plants and soil life. By planting native flowers, you invite native butterflies, bees and predatory insects that feed on the abundance of nectar and troublesome critters. In return, they assist you with pollinating your vegetables and managing pests. It's especially beneficial to the native wildlife because their homes are constantly under threat by human development and large agriculture operations.

Whether you have a garden to grow your own food or for sheer floral pleasure, watering your garden can be a lot of work and costly if tending to a larger garden. That's why I was so pleasantly surprised when I learned that native plants are easier, and much more cost effective, to water. Taking care of exotic or foreign plants in the garden can be quite demanding. You have to mimic the conditions of their own natural habitat. It can take tons of water to mirror the damp forest floor high in the Japanese mountains. Yes, the flowers may be beautiful, but it will take a substantial amount of care to keep such plants happy. The beauty of planting native plants is that they'll already be accustomed to the water conditions in your region. For example, if you're in an area that can experience droughts, the native plants

An Eastern Tiger Swallowtail feeding on the nectar of a native Joe Pye Weed. I've observed that native plants are typically far more loaded with pollinators than foreign or cultivated varieties of plants. >

will have adapted to hold more water and endure dry spells. Of course, watering them will still be of great benefit to them, but it's not nearly as much of a life-or-death situation if you forget to water or only give them a light shower. Native plants can handle it.

Another strenuous task in the garden can be staking or protecting your plants during extreme weather conditions, meaning you'll be a lot more stressed over a plant rather than really being able to enjoy it. Well, guess

Asclepias tuberosa, *also know as the Butterfly Milkweed, in varying blooming stages. It is native to North America.*

what? You won't have to worry nearly as much about the weather conditions in your area with native plants; they're designed to handle it. For example, here in Tennessee, we have tons of beautiful native plants that overwinter and can come back year after year. Many of them can also withstand intense winds because they have adapted to do so. Whenever you plant a native in the garden, that's one less worry you'll have.

Planting exotic flowers in the garden allows for beautiful scenery, but it also invites the potential for opportunistic or invasive plants to take over. Introducing foreign species can have major impacts on the ecology of your region. I mentioned earlier how some plants may need more care to survive in your conditions, but some plants can actually thrive. So much so that they can overrun and choke out native species, disrupting the natural balance of the ecosystem. Disrupting native plants can cause a chain reaction that affects the birds, insects and other creatures that depend on them. Planting native plants doesn't just minimize that risk; it encourages the sustainability of native wildlife.

As you can see, there are a myriad of benefits to planting natives. Whether it's in your garden, back porch or balcony, planting native flowers is a great way to encourage the native wildlife and help sustain their natural habitats. It takes gardening and growing beyond the point of just self-gratifying satisfaction. It makes it far more intentional, purposeful and fulfilling, knowing that we can grow something so beautiful that will also benefit the native creatures.

I recommend researching which plants are native to your area or state. I was so happy to discover the beautiful varieties that are native here to Tennessee, such as elderberry, anise hyssop, common milkweed and even a few varieties of bee balm! It really opens the door to creating a unique and sustainable garden. I'm not completely bashing on planting exotic plants, either; I still plant them, too, but it's important to be conscious of the balance you have in the garden when mixing native and exotic plants. Balance is the key.

Eryngium yuccifolium, *also know as rattlesnake Master. It is native to North America.*

Maximizing Your Space: Companion Planting and Interplanting

You would be surprised at how well plants can actually grow together and how much you can squeeze in a small amount of space. To get the most out of your space, you can master the ways of companion planting and interplanting. These techniques have been used for centuries to enhance the productivity and health of gardens. They involve placing certain plants together in a way that benefits both plants.

Companion planting refers to the practice of juxtaposing two or more varieties of plants that benefit one another in some way, by repelling pests, enhancing flavor or providing shade, while also being attractive together. For example, planting marigolds alongside tomatoes can help repel harmful insects while also creating a beautiful contrast of colors.

The vegetable garden in early summer. Pay attention to the deep interplanting of flowering plants, grasses, herbs and vegetables to create an incredible biodiverse ecosystem.

Interplanting, on the other hand, refers to the practice of planting two or more crops in the same space, often in a way that maximizes use of the available sunlight, soil nutrients and water. For example, planting lettuce and radishes together can help maximize the use of soil space and light, since lettuce grows tall and radishes are short.

There are many examples of companion planting and interplanting that have proven to be successful in gardens all over the world. Here are just a few:

- *Tomatoes and basil:* Planting basil alongside tomatoes can help repel harmful insects while improving the flavor of the tomatoes.

- *Carrots and onions:* Planting onions alongside carrots can help repel carrot flies while providing a tasty companion for your next meal.

- *Cucumbers and nasturtiums:* Planting nasturtiums alongside cucumbers can help repel cucumber beetles while providing a beautiful contrast in color.

- *Lettuce and radishes:* Planting radishes alongside lettuce can help maximize the use of soil space and light while also providing a tasty and colorful addition to your salad.

More examples of heavy interplanting to increase biodiversity, which helps maintain pest populations, attract pollinators and maximize the potential of a space.

The Three Sisters

One of the most famous examples of the companion planting technique is the Three Sisters, a Native American grouping of three complementary crops—corn, beans and squash. It is called "sisters" because each crop contributes to the growth of the others, much in the way siblings work together to thrive.

First, corn is planted in a mound, with a few seeds in each mound. When the corn is around 6 inches (15 cm) tall, the second crop, beans, is planted around the base of the corn. The beans then grow up the corn-stalks, providing support for the corn and adding nitrogen to the soil. Finally, squash is planted around the beans and corn, where it acts as a living mulch, keeping the soil moist and weed-free.

The key to success with the Three Sisters is timing. The corn must be planted first so that it can be both tall enough to actually support the beans once it takes off and not get completely shrouded by the large leaves of the squash. I'd recommend sowing beans 4 to 6 inches (10 to 15 cm) away from the corn once it's over a foot (30 cm) tall, then directly sow your squash 4 to 5 feet (1.2 to 1.5 m) away once the beans have taken hold. It may seem far, but squash will crawl its way over in no time. These are all hot crops, so only start them after the risk of frost has passed.

An example of how pole beans climb the corn, using their stalks for support.

These are just a few examples of the many successful companion plant combinations that can be used in your garden. By planting in this way, you can squeeze every last bit of abundance out of your space. Something else that I found so exciting about companion planting and interplanting is you discover just how versatile plants can really be. Once you get a sense of how certain plants grow and the influence they can have over other plants, you can start experimenting with your very own combinations! As long as you don't plant plants that don't vibe next to each other, the possibilities are endless.

A Guide for Companions

Marigolds

When I first planted marigolds, they pleasantly surprised me. Marigolds are not just beautiful flowers that add color and vibrancy to your garden; they are also an excellent companion plant for a variety of other plants. Marigolds are easy to grow, low maintenance and can be planted throughout the growing season.

Preferred Conditions: Marigolds are hardy annuals and can thrive in growing zones 2 to 11. They prefer full sun to partial shade and well-draining soil. Marigolds can be sown directly into the ground or started indoors and transplanted outdoors after the last frost. When planting marigolds, be sure to give them enough space to grow, as they can grow up to 3 feet (91 cm) high.

Role in the Garden: One of the most significant benefits of planting marigolds in your garden is that they produce a strong aroma that can deter such pests as aphids, whiteflies and nematodes from attacking nearby plants. Additionally, marigolds can attract beneficial insects, such as ladybugs, lacewings and hoverflies, which can help control other pests in your garden. Marigolds are also great for improving soil health. They release a chemical called alpha-terthienyl, which is toxic to harmful soil-borne organisms, such as root-knot nematodes. This chemical also promotes the growth of beneficial microorganisms in the soil.

Ideal Companions: Tomatoes, peppers, eggplants, squash, corn and basil.

Dill

Dill is one of my favorite culinary herbs, but also one of my favorite companion plants in the garden!

Preferred Conditions: This versatile herb is an annual plant that grows in zones 2 to 11. It thrives in full sun, well-drained soil and with consistent moisture. I always recommend directly sowing dill seeds after your final frost date and thinning them out as they grow. Be sure to give them ample space because they can get tall, reaching heights of up to 3 to 4 feet (91 cm to 1.22 m).

Role in the Garden: Dill is an excellent companion plant for a variety of garden vegetables, as it helps repel pests and attract beneficial insects. More specifically, it attracts a parasitic wasp that preys on cabbage worms, making it an ideal companion for members of the brassica family, such as cabbage, cauliflower and kale. Dill is also a host plant for swallowtail butterflies; I'm always finding their caterpillars munching away at the growing leaves.

Ideal Companions: Brassicas, leafy greens, tomatoes, peppers, eggplants, cucumbers, squash, beans and potatoes.

Nasturtiums

One of my favorite companions in the garden! Nasturtiums have a plethora of benefits in the garden—and they're edible! Nasturtium flowers make a beautiful topper for salads or a drink and add a floral, spicy kick.

Preferred Conditions: These hardy annuals can grow in zones 2 to 11. Planting nasturtiums is relatively easy. They prefer well-draining soil and full sun, but can also tolerate some shade. Nasturtiums can be grown from seeds, which can be sown directly into the ground or started indoors and transplanted after final frost. It helps to soak their seeds for 24 hours before planting.

Role in the Garden: Nasturtiums produce a strong fragrance that repels many pests, including aphids, whiteflies and squash bugs. They also attract beneficial insects, such as ladybugs and bees, which help pollinate other plants in your garden. Ladybugs in particular are very effective in managing aphids, one of their favorite things to eat! Ladybugs are substantial eaters, but their larvae can consume more than 10 times as much as adults can. Nasturtiums also have a unique ability to improve soil health. Their roots release a substance that inhibits the growth of harmful bacteria in the soil, while also providing a habitat for beneficial bacteria. This helps create a healthier and more diverse soil environment, which can lead to improved plant growth.

Ideal Companions: Brassicas, tomatoes, peppers, eggplants, cucumbers, squash, beans, corn and basil.

Calendula

Calendula, also known as pot marigold, is a beloved and versatile plant that serves not only as a decorative addition to the garden, but also as a helpful companion to many other plants.

Preferred Conditions: Calendula is a hardy annual grown in zones 2 to 11. It prefers full sun to partial shade and well-draining soil. When planting calendula, it is best to sow the seeds thinly, as they can grow quite vigorously. The plant prefers well-draining soil but should be watered regularly to keep the soil consistently moist.

Role in the Garden: One of the reasons calendula is a great companion plant is that it attracts beneficial insects, such as bees, butterflies and hoverflies, to the garden. These insects help pollinate other plants and control pests, such as aphids and spider mites. Additionally, calendula's strong scent repels many harmful pests, making it a natural pest deterrent. Calendula also has a beneficial effect on the soil. Its deep taproot can break up compacted soil, and its fallen leaves provide nutrients as they decompose. The plant's extensive root system also helps retain moisture in the soil, making it an excellent companion for plants that prefer a consistently moist environment.

Ideal Companions: Brassicas, leafy greens, tomatoes, peppers, eggplants, cucumbers, squash, beans and corn.

Beans

Beans are one of the most versatile and beneficial plants to grow in your garden, and they make fantastic companion plants for numerous reasons.

Preferred Conditions: Beans come in many different varieties and are suitable for a wide range of hardiness zones, from 3 to 11. However, it is important to choose the right type of bean for your particular conditions. Some popular kinds of beans include pole beans, which need a vertical support, and bush beans, which stay pretty compact. When planting beans, it is important to choose a site that receives full sun and has well-drained soil. It is always recommended to direct sow beans, as they have very sensitive root systems and perform best when left undisturbed. Beans love the heat, so be sure to plant them after the risk of frost has passed.

Role in the Garden: Beans are legumes, which means that they have the ability to fix nitrogen in the soil, making it more available to other plants. Their versatility as either a vining or bush plant allows them to be interplanted in a wide variety of ways. This makes them an excellent choice for companion planting with other vegetables that require a lot of nitrogen, such as corn or tomatoes. Beans can also attract beneficial insects, such as bees and ladybugs, which help pollinate other plants and control harmful pests. Talk about a powerhouse in the garden!

Ideal Companions: Brassicas, tomatoes, peppers, eggplants, cucumbers, squash, corn and potatoes.

Garlic

Oh, garlic, the mighty bulb that not only brings flavor and nutrition to our meals but also wards off pests in the garden.

Preferred Conditions: Garlic is a hardy plant that can thrive in a wide range of growing conditions, and it's generally recommended for hardiness zones 3 to 9. It's an easy grower and doesn't take up much space, so it's very versatile to place among your other crops. Ideally, you plant garlic in the late fall, for a summer harvest, but you can do it throughout the season just for its beneficial effects in the garden. Garlic prefers full sun and well-drained soil.

Role in the Garden: Garlic is a great companion plant because it repels such pests as aphids, spider mites and cabbage loopers. It also has antibacterial and antifungal properties, which can help prevent diseases in neighboring plants.

Ideal Companions: Brassicas, tomatoes, peppers and squash.

Onions

Onions! I don't go a single day without onions involved. Onions are not only a delicious addition to many meals, but they are also great companions in the garden.

Preferred Conditions: Onions are generally hardy in zones 3 to 9, depending on their variety. They prefer well-draining soil and full sun, and should be planted in the spring or fall. Their compact growth habit makes them very easy plants to intermingle among other crops.

Role in the Garden: Onions help repel many garden pests, such as aphids, carrot flies and cabbage worms, as well as help suppress fungal diseases in the soil.

Ideal Companions: Brassicas, tomatoes, peppers, beans, carrots and squash.

Carrots

The beloved garden staple, and for good reason. Not only are carrots delicious and nutritious, but they also make fantastic companion plants in the garden.

Preferred Conditions: Carrots are a cool season crop and are typically grown in zones 3 to 10. They're happiest when planted in early spring or early fall in deep, fluffy soil. Their compact nature makes them very easy to sprinkle in between other plants. For continued abundance throughout the season, succession plant them every few weeks. Direct sow seeds and thin them out so they're at least 3 inches (7.5 cm) apart.

Role in the Garden: Carrots make wonderful companions because they have a relatively small root system that doesn't compete with other crops. They also attract beneficial insects, such as ladybugs, lacewings and hoverflies, which help control pests in the garden. Carrots also help improve soil health by releasing nutrients into the soil and breaking up compacted soil.

Ideal Companions: Brassicas, tomatoes, peppers, beans, onions, radishes and squash.

Putting a hand to the largest cabbage ever grown at Redleaf.>

Chapter 9

Seed Starting 101

To Sow or Not to Sow

Starting seedlings is one of my greatest passions in the realm of gardening. The entire process fascinates me: preparing the soil that will house the seeds, meeting the diverse offspring of countless plants, tucking the seeds underneath the soil, watching the first cotyledons, or the first leaves to appear from a sprouting seed, emerge from the seed as they reach for light, witnessing the first true leaves—a glimpse of what the plant will really look like—and caring for them until it's time to introduce them to the garden.

There is quite a bit to understand about seeds and seedlings to be able to successfully nurture them. They grow in different conditions and have evolved to thrive in said conditions. Their growing habits, their flowers, their roots, the relationships they've formed with other creatures in their environment—and their seeds—have all been specifically crafted to exist perfectly in their environment. That being said, every plant has different needs when it comes to successfully germinating its offspring. Some are easily satisfied, whereas others require months of ice-cold temperatures, stratification (treating seeds to simulate naturally occurring conditions) or even fermentation. To get the best understanding of how a plant likes to grow, study its environment and the conditions that led to the creation of the plant before you.

When it comes to starting seeds for your garden, make sure you know the conditions and soil requirements that those seeds need to be able to germinate. The conditions vary from plant to plant, but the means of starting seeds can be broken into two categories: *direct sowing* or *starting indoors*.

Direct Sowing

Some plants have very delicate root systems and can experience shock if they're disturbed in the slightest. That is why it's best for some plants to be direct sown in the garden exactly where you intend to grow them for the season. Once the seeds have sprouted and are forming roots, they should no longer be moved. They want to set their roots right where they land, so keep that in mind when planning your garden and once you've sown your seeds. If moved, the shock can be so severe that it can stunt their growth or even kill them. I wish I knew all of this before starting dozens of corn, bean and squash seeds my first year of growing. You could imagine my disappointment when they refused to acclimate to the new conditions and chose to die instead. The shock was too much for them to bear and they failed to thrive.

When sowing seeds, a few important things to pay attention to are the depth that the seeds want to be planted, the kind of soil they need and the time of year when they should be sown. The depth of the seeds is critical and can make or break successful germination. Some seeds prefer to be planted deep into the ground, cradled by the soil. Others prefer to be sown directly onto the Earth where they can be exposed to all the elements. The type of soil plays a significant role in germination as well. Some seeds do well in soil that remains loose but can still hold a lot of moisture; others in sandier or rocky soil with sharp drainage. Finally, note the time of year with regard to planting seeds. Some seeds will only germinate if temperatures are consistently around or above 70°F (21°C), whereas others need to be planted in the fall so they can stratify overwinter.

When you directly sow your seedlings outdoors, it's important to properly care for them so that they can successfully germinate, by ensuring the soil around them remains moist, has proper exposure to light and is protected by a fine layer of mulch from any critters looking for a snack. Once the seeds actually sprout, make sure they are well watered. You never want your babies to dry out, especially in their most vulnerable stage of development. One great benefit of directly sowing your seedlings outdoors is that they will start their life already exposed to the conditions of Nature, such as direct sunlight and fluctuations in temperature, humidity and gusts of wind. Seeds started indoors are at a slight disadvantage because they need to be properly acclimated to the real-world conditions before being transplanted in the ground through a process called *hardening off*.

Starting Seeds Indoors

Why even start seedlings indoors, then? Well, if the plant is tough enough, starting seedlings indoors with the intention of transplanting them outdoors is a great way of getting a head start on their growth for the season. This is especially beneficial for flowering and fruiting plants that require a few extra months of growth that can't be met outdoors due to colder temperatures. For example, if you live in a cooler zone, you'd want to start tomatoes indoors two months before your final frost of the winter season, so your tomato plants have ample time during the growing season to actually produce enough fruit for you to harvest. If you were to direct sow them outdoors after frost, you'd be two months behind on their growth and they may not have enough time to produce fruit for you, especially if you have a shorter season. The same rings true for flowering plants; you want to give them a head start so you can actually enjoy their floral display during the season. The factors you would pay attention to when planting outdoors also come into play when starting seeds indoors. Make sure you pay attention to the depth seeds need to be planted, the soil medium you're using and the time of year you're planting them.

Allow me to walk you through the steps I take when starting my seedlings indoors:

1. **Prepare the pots or trays.** Depending on what I'm planting, I like to prepare 2-inch (5-cm) pots or trays with smaller cells by filling them about two-thirds of the way with my seed-starting soil mix. I'm sure to get a seed starter mix because it's free of fertilizers that the seedlings wouldn't necessarily need at this stage. All the nutrients they need to get started are actually all packed up in the husk of the seed and acquired through photosynthesis. I'm sure to leave the upper third of the pot empty so that it can be filled in at a later stage if my seedlings get leggy. The soil I add would provide extra support to their little stems.

2. **Sow the seeds.** Once my pots and cell trays are ready for planting, I place two or three seeds on the soil. I like to use more than one seed, to increase the chances of successful germination. If more than one seedling sprouts, they can be thinned out or divided later on.

3. **Bury the seeds, if needed.** Depending on the seeds and how deeply they want to be buried in the soil, I sprinkle in the appropriate amount of soil needed to cover them. If a seed wants to be surface sown, I don't bury it in at all.

4. **Gently water the seeds.** Use a mister or a mist setting on a watering hose to gently water your seeds. Seeds act as a little sponge that absorbs the water and kick-starts the germination process. Keep the soil moist at all times; you do not want your seeds or seedlings to dry out. One of the perks of leaving extra room in your pots or cell trays is that your seeds, especially the ones that want to be sown on the surface, won't spill out from the edges if watered too heavily. They'll all stay safe and secure in their pot.

5. **Provide the seeds with ideal conditions until they germinate.** I'm starting my seedlings in a very warm greenhouse, so the conditions are ideal for germination. The temperature stays consistently around 70°F (21°C), the air remains humid and the light is bright and diffused through a thick layer of white plastic overhead. If you want to match these conditions in your home, start your seeds next to a windowsill or on a rack with grow lights. Consistently spritz your seeds to keep them moist or place them under a humidity dome. I've even seen people cut a gallon-sized (3.8-L) jug in half and use it to make a mini greenhouse, which keeps the seeds and seedlings warm and moist until it's time to repot or transplant them.

6. **Be patient.** Some seeds are quick to germinate, but some can take a few weeks.

7. **Once the seedlings sprout, take good care of your babies.** As discussed, keep well watered, but not too moist. I like to let them dry a bit between waterings to toughen them up. Give them plenty of light and fill the remainder of the pot with soil if seedlings get too leggy. This means the seedlings grow a long, fragile stem as they attempt to reach for the available light. These delicate stems make it easy for the plant to potentially snap, so it's best to give them the support they need. I wait a few days until the seedlings have grown nice and strong before going in and thinning an overabundance of seedlings or dividing them. Be very, very careful when dividing seedlings, as you want to cause them the least possible disturbance. To thin seedlings, I simply use slender trimmers to cut the unwanted seedlings at the base. I leave the strongest-growing seedling and feed the soil with the trimmed foliage. To prepare them for windy conditions outdoors, I've seen growers place an oscillating fan by their seedlings to expose them to wind and toughen their stems.

8. **Repot the seedlings.** If you started your seedlings in a larger container or pot, this might not be necessary. Although these plants may be tougher than ones that need to be direct sown, you still don't want to cause much disturbance to the roots. If you start seeds in smaller cells, they will come to a point when they'll need repotting to grow larger and stronger before going outdoors. A few signs a plant needs to be repotted are finding roots coming out of the bottom of the pot or the soil beginning to dry too quickly. The larger the plant, the more water it needs. When repotting, you want to rehome the plant in a pot that's twice as large as the one it was in before.

A freshly transplanted pepper seedling.

Hardening Off Seedlings

Once the weather allows for transplanting outdoors, it is vital that you harden off your seedlings before transferring them to the garden. I learned this the hard way my first year of growing. All the hard work that went into caring for my seedlings scorched up in a single day. When you grow seedlings indoors, they become accustomed to the consistent conditions that you provide. They have never experienced extreme shifts in temperature, gusts of wind or direct sunlight. That means we have to gently train them to withstand these new conditions. The process may be a bit tedious, but it's worth not losing all the seedlings you worked so hard to grow.

Ideally, you want to begin the hardening process two weeks before you plan to move them outside and when temperatures are consistently above 50°F (10°C). To get started, find a shaded area with enough room to support your seedlings. Once you find an ideal shaded location, place your seedlings in that area for one hour, making sure to keep a close eye for any scorching of the leaves or too harsh an exposure to wind. You'll know your leaves are scorching if the leaves start lightening in color, almost as if getting bleached. After the first hour, bring them back indoors. On the second day, you will repeat this process, but you will leave them in the shaded area for two hours, then bring them back indoors. On the third day, you repeat the process, but for three hours. On the fourth day, go for four hours and so on. By the end of the first week, your seedlings should be able to endure at least six hours of being outside in the shaded area. The following week, on the eighth day, it's time to introduce them to direct sunlight. Only do this if the seedlings you're planting need full sun to thrive. If the seedlings prefer shade, do not expose them to the sun. Place your seedlings in the sun for just one hour and keep a close eye on them for signs of scorching on their leaves. If scorching does happen, do not be alarmed. It's very common for the older leaves to experience some scorching. What you want to pay attention to are the newest leaves. As they acclimate to the sun, they should come in green and strong. After an hour, bring them back indoors. Repeat the process throughout the week, increasing the exposure to sunlight by an hour each day. Play close attention during the sun-exposure phase to make sure your seedlings don't dry out. The warmth of the sun will cause the soil to heat more quickly and any remaining water to evaporate. Try to water your seedlings from below or directly into the pot. Any water droplets on the leaves can cause the sunlight to refract and burn their tender skin, similar to a magnifying glass. During the hardening process, they will also be getting exposed to wind, so you may also notice their stems thickening up and growing more fortified. By the end of the second week, your seedlings should be able to endure a full day outdoors in full sun. Once you're confident that your seedlings are well acclimated to the outdoor conditions, it's time to transplant them in the garden.

When it's time to rehome your seedlings, make sure that the hole they're going in is twice the width and depth of the pot that the seedling was growing in. I like to throw in a spadeful of compost and a handful of organic fertilizer to ensure the seedlings have all the nutrients they need to get established. Every seedling has different watering requirements, so pay close attention to whether the soil below is still moist or not, then water accordingly.

There is no greater sense of fulfillment than growing your precious plants from their most tender stage to strong, mature specimens. I'm always amazed that something so petite can house such tremendous potential for life, bringing forth the abundance of their flowers, fruits and potentially hundreds of more offspring. Mastering the art of seed starting relinquishes the dependency on external sources to grow your abundance, and if you're anything like me, you'll end up with an overflow of precious plants that you can share.

Lilium leichtinii blooming in July.

Chapter 10

The Abundance Plant Guide

Through my ventures in the garden, I've developed a deep understanding and relationship with all the plants that I grow. I now know what the plants I enjoy growing need to thrive. Allow me to share with you the many plants that I grow and how I grow them to reap their delicious abundance.

The Easy Growers

Here is a small collection of plants that I've found to be very easy growers in the garden. I've had huge success with these plants and would highly recommend them to beginners.

Mizuna

A unique leafy green closely related to mustard, delicious and nutritious with a peppery kick very reminiscent of arugula. A green revered in Japan for its numerous health benefits, including a richness of antioxidants.

Preferred Conditions: Hardiness zones 4 to 9; prefers cooler temperatures. A wonderful spring and fall crop. Frost hardy.

Planting Method: Direct sow two weeks before your final frost date.

Light: Full sun to part shade.

Basil

One of the most commonly grown herbs used in cuisine all over the world. It is also loved in the garden by pollinators when given the chance to flower. Makes a great companion as well, repelling numerous pests.

Preferred Conditions: Hardiness zones 4 to 9 as an annual, zones 10 to 13 as a perennial. Not frost hardy.

Planting Method: Transplant or direct sow after final frost.

Light: Full sun.

Sorrel

A scrumptious and nutritious leafy green with a refreshing, tangy crunch. A very tough and hardy grower in the garden that can provide abundance for many years. Harvest often for salads, soups and more.

Preferred Conditions: Hardiness zones 3 to 9 and perennial. Frost hardy.

Planting Method: Transplant or direct sow two weeks before final frost.

Light: Full sun to part shade.

Summer Squash

A productive staple in many kitchen gardens. Has large bushing or vining habits, so make sure you have ample room for your squash plants to extend. For the most abundance, plant in loose, rich soil; they're heavy eaters and quick growers.

Preferred Conditions: Hardiness zones 3 to 10. Not frost hardy.

Planting Method: Direct sow after final frost.

Light: Full sun.

Beans

Nature's powerhouse! Beans offer many uses in cuisine and the garden. A great companion plant known for fixing nitrogen within the soil. They grow in a bushing or vining habit, so offer them vertical support.

Preferred Conditions: Hardiness zones 2 to 11. There are annual and perennial varieties.

Planting Method: Direct sow after final frost. Not frost hardy.

Light: Full sun.

Peppers

One of the most productive fruits in the garden! There are thousands of varieties with a dazzling array of deliciously sweet to scorching hot flavors.

Preferred Conditions: Hardiness zones 3 to 9 as annuals. Hardiness zones 10 to 13 as perennials. A true summer crop. Not frost hardy.

Planting Method: Transplant after final frost in rich, loamy soil.

Light: Full sun.

Kale

A cruciferous green known for its crisp and hardy bite. Kale is related to cabbages, cauliflower and broccoli, meaning it loves cooler growing climates. Some varieties can grow very large, so be sure you space it well.

Preferred Conditions: Hardiness zones 4 to 9. Frost hardy.

Planting Method: Transplant or direct sow two weeks before final frost.

Light: Full sun to part shade.

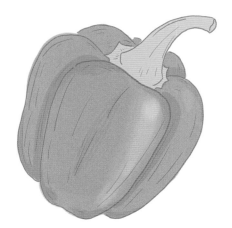

Lettuce

Their crunchy, slightly sweet leaves make lettuce a popular addition to many dishes. A fairly hardy grower that prefers the cooler and wetter months.

Preferred Conditions: Hardiness zones 2 to 11. Frost hardy.

Planting Method: Transplant or direct sow two weeks before final frost.

Light: Full sun to part shade.

Carrots

A nutrient-rich root vegetable that comes in a variety of shapes, sizes and colors. An easy early spring grower that is great to interplant among tomatoes.

Preferred Conditions: Hardiness zones 3 to 10; prefers cooler weather. A great spring and fall crop. Frost hardy.

Planting Method: Direct sow seeds two weeks before final frost. Sprinkle seeds in long trenches or groupings within loose, well-draining soil. Be sure to thin seedlings to 2 to 3 inches (5 to 7.5 cm) apart once they start growing.

Light: Full sun to part shade.

Sunflowers

With dozens of different varieties to choose from, you can fill your gardens with towering guardians or bushing bursts of color. Sunflowers offer an abundance of seeds for you and the birds.

Preferred Conditions: Hardiness zones 4 to 10. There are annual and perennial varieties.

Planting Method: Direct sow after final frost. Not frost hardy.

Light: Full sun.

A Purple Dragon carrot being plucked from the garden. >

The Cool Crops— Plants for Spring and Fall

Let's talk cool crops! For reference, I am growing in zone 7b, so these are the practices I've learned growing this array of crops in my specific conditions. That being said, growing any plant will vary from garden to garden, but the fundamental truths of what each plant wants so it can thrive remain the same.

As the name suggests, cool crops prefer cooler temperatures ranging from 55 to 75°F (13 to 24°C). They grow their best in the spring and fall, where they can still get ample amounts of sunlight without the overwhelming heat. Cool crops, such as leafy greens and brassicas, are prized for their crisp leaves and cruciferous buds. Intense heat causes them to *bolt*, meaning they go to flower, and when they do so, their leaves and overall flavor become much more bitter. Brassicas actually get sweeter in colder temperatures as well.

It's worth noting that most cool crops are typically *frost hardy*, meaning they can withstand below freezing temperatures. If the forecast warns of consistently below-freezing weather, though, it would be best to harvest what you have left. They can withstand the cold to an extent, but too frequent bone-chilling conditions will eventually cause some damage. Root vegetables, on the other hand, are better equipped to withstand the cold, since most of their growing happens underground. I've come back to prepare beds in the spring to find carrots still growing, surviving the few cold months of winter.

Now that you've been briefly introduced to cool crops, let's dive deeper into their preferred growing conditions.

Brassicas

Kale

In my opinion, kale is one of the easiest plants to grow in a garden. There are many varieties to choose from, coming in a wide array of textures and colors. They are a member of the brassica family, meaning they are closely related to cauliflower, broccoli and cabbage. They grow best in well-drained, fertile soil. Brassicas are primarily grown for their foliage, so for best results, feed them well with a nitrogen-rich fertilizer. Nitrogen is what helps the greenery of plants grow its best.

Preferred Conditions: Grown as an annual in zones 2 to 6. Can grow year-round in zones 7 to 10. Kale enjoys frequent waterings so the soil remains moist. Frost hardy.

Spacing: 18 to 24 inches (45 to 61 cm) apart.

Planting Method: Transplant or direct sow two weeks before your final frost date for spring planting, or three months before first frost for fall planting. Make sure to stay on top of watering if planting in late summer for fall.

Light: Full sun.

Companion Plants: Beets, onions, peas, potatoes, lettuce, spinach, dill, rosemary, garlic, hyssop, marigolds, nasturtiums.

Broccoli & Cauliflower

Popular cool crops grown for their delicious cruciferous buds. When we eat cauliflower and broccoli, what we're actually eating are the flower buds before they bolt and go to bloom. You could also eat their tender leaves. They grow best in well-drained, fertile soil. For best results, feed them well with a nitrogen-rich fertilizer. They generally take three to five months from sowing to maturity, but growth rates vary according to the variety and weather conditions. Here in Tennessee, my brassicas are targeted by the pesky cabbage worm. I always advocate for organic growing, so rather than spraying chemicals, I build cages around my brassicas with a mesh cloth to keep the cabbage worms at bay.

Preferred Conditions: Growing zones 2 to 10, depending on the variety. They enjoy frequent waterings so the soil remains moist. Frost hardy.

Spacing: 24 inches (61 cm) apart.

Planting Method: Transplant or direct sow two weeks before your final frost date for spring planting, or three months before first frost for fall planting. Make sure to stay on top of watering if planting in late summer for fall.

Light: Full sun.

Companion Plants: Beets, onions, peas, potatoes, lettuce, spinach, dill, rosemary, garlic, hyssop, marigolds, nasturtiums.

Cabbage

One of the most rewarding cool crops to grow. Some varieties can get massive, so be sure you have the space. They grow best in well-drained, fertile soil. For best results, feed them well with a nitrogen-rich fertilizer. Cabbage comes to harvest in 80 to 180 days from seed or in 60 to 105 days from transplants, depending upon the variety. Flavor improves in colder temperatures.

Preferred Conditions: Growing zones 1 to 10, depending on the variety. They enjoy frequent waterings so the soil remains moist. Frost hardy.

Spacing: 24 to 36 inches (61 to 91 cm) apart.

Planting Method: Transplant or direct sow two weeks before your final frost date for spring planting, or three months before first frost for fall planting. Make sure to stay on top of watering if planting in late summer for fall.

Light: Full sun.

Companion Plants: Beets, onions, peas, potatoes, lettuce, spinach, dill, rosemary, garlic, hyssop, marigolds, nasturtiums, geraniums.

Leafy Greens

Lettuce

A quick grower and very abundant. Lettuces don't take up that much space or nutrients, so they make a great companion to interplant among larger, slower-growing plants. There are many varieties to choose from so a salad will never get boring. Harvest often and they will continue to produce more.

Preferred Conditions: Growing zones 2 to 11, depending on the variety. They enjoy frequent waterings so the soil remains moist. Frost hardy.

Spacing: 6 to 18 inches (15 to 45 cm) apart.

Planting Method: Direct sow two weeks before your final frost date for spring planting, or two months before first frost for fall planting. Make sure to stay on top of watering if planting in late summer for fall.

Light: Full sun to part shade.

Companion Plants: Beets, onions, carrots, brassicas, spinach, beans, tomatoes, nasturtiums, strawberries.

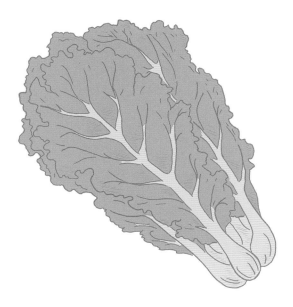

Spinach

One of the most popular leafy greens to grow in the garden. Harvest frequently for more abundance. Another crop that makes a great companion to larger growing plants.

Preferred Conditions: Growing zones 2 to 9, depending on the variety. They enjoy frequent waterings so the soil remains moist. Frost hardy.

Spacing: 8 to 12 inches (20 to 30 cm) apart.

Planting Method: Direct sow two weeks before your final frost date for spring planting, or two months before first frost for fall planting. Make sure to stay on top of watering if planting in late summer for fall.

Light: Full sun to part shade.

Companion Plants: Onions, carrots, brassicas, lettuce, beans, peas, chard, tomatoes, nasturtiums, zinnias, cosmos, strawberries.

Chard

An abundant and hardy grower that comes in a dazzling array of varieties. In warmer climates, chard can be grown year-round. Grows well in containers, too.

Preferred Conditions: Growing zones 3 to 10, depending on the variety. They enjoy frequent waterings so the soil remains moist. Frost hardy.

Spacing: 8 to 12 inches (20 to 30 cm) apart.

Planting Method: Direct sow or transplant two weeks before your final frost date for spring planting, or two months before first frost for fall planting. Make sure to stay on top of watering if planting in late summer for fall.

Light: Full sun to part shade.

Companion Plants: Onions, carrots, brassicas, lettuce, beans, peas, tomatoes, nasturtiums, zinnias, cosmos, calendula, strawberries.

Root Veggies

Carrots

One of my favorite things to grow in the garden! Every pluck provides a crunchy, unexpected surprise. They're relatively light feeders and don't take up a lot of room, so they make great companions. Their green tops are also edible. Depending on the variety, carrots can take two to four months to mature.

Preferred Conditions: Growing zones 3 to 10, depending on the variety. Some can even overwinter. They enjoy moist, loose and well-drained soil. Frost hardy.

Spacing: 2 to 3 inches (5 to 7.5 cm) apart. Direct sow seeds in large groupings. Once the seedlings have sprouted and grown to be 3 inches (7.5 cm) in height, pluck and thin the thick grouping of seedlings so the remaining sprouts have at least 3 inches (7.5 cm) between them. If left to grow too close, you'll end up with some split or funny looking carrots.

Planting Method: Direct sow two weeks before your final frost date for spring planting, or two months before first frost for fall planting. Make sure to stay on top of watering if planting in late summer for fall.

Light: Full sun to part shade.

Companion Plants: Tomatoes, peppers, eggplants, cabbage, kale, onions, peas, rosemary, marigolds, nasturtiums.

Beets

A powerhouse veggie with edible leaves and roots. It's considered a superfood and comes in many shapes, sizes and colors.

Preferred Conditions: Growing zones 2 to 11, depending on the variety. They enjoy moist, loose and well-drained soil. Frost hardy.

Spacing: Their "seed" is actually a cluster of three to six seeds. Direct sow and thin seedlings when they're 2 inches (5 cm) tall so that they're 4 to 5 inches (10 to 12.5 cm) apart.

Planting Method: Direct sow two weeks before your final frost date for spring planting, or two months before first frost for fall planting. Make sure to stay on top of watering if planting in late summer for fall. For increased germination, soak seeds for 24 hours before planting.

Light: Full sun to part shade.

Companion Plants: Cabbage, cauliflower, lettuce, onions, corn.

Potatoes

Potaaatoes! One of the things I love most in the garden is getting to roll around in dirt—and one of the dirtiest jobs is harvesting potatoes! What joy I feel from shoving my hand deep underground and pulling out an abundance of potatoes. I plant a few varieties each year and am always thrilled to see the rainbow harvest. They're also pretty heavy feeders, so throw on a layer of compost wherever you're planting your potatoes.

Preferred Conditions: Growing zones 3 to 10. For best results, plant in a deep bed with loose, rich, well-drained soil. Many growers plant them in rows and build mounds over them as the stems grow. Keep them covered with earth so the potatoes don't go green, which creates solanine, a toxic substance.

Spacing: 12 to 24 inches (30 to 61 cm) apart.

Planting Method: Direct sow seed potatoes two weeks before your final frost for a summer harvest. You can even plant in midfall so they can overwinter and get a head start growing in the spring.

Light: Full sun.

Companion Plants: Brassicas, lettuce, spinach, beans, peas, chamomile, thyme, marigolds, nasturtiums.

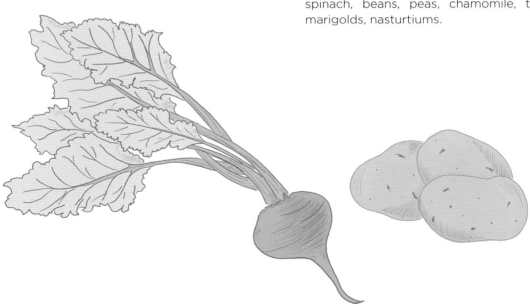

An abundant mid-summer potato harvest.

Onions

A staple in my kitchen. They're heavy feeders, so be sure to apply a fresh layer of compost before planting. A great companion in the garden, known to repel many unwanted pests.

Preferred Conditions: Onions are categorized into three groups: short-day, intermediate and long-day. Short-day onions do best in zones 6 to 11; intermediates do best in 5 to 7; long-days do best in zones 1 to 5.

Spacing: 4 to 6 inches (10 to 15 cm) apart.

Planting Method: Start seedlings indoors six to eight weeks before final frost and transplant in early spring. Bulbs can be planted in early spring for a midsummer harvest or in early fall. Once established, onions can even overwinter.

Light: Full sun.

Companion Plants: Brassicas, lettuce, beets, carrots, tomatoes, peppers, eggplant, squash, melons, strawberries, chamomile.

Garlic! The Winter Crop

The crop that gets me through the winter. When it's cold and gray out, I can get my garden fix by watching my garlic grow. It takes garlic eight to nine months to fully mature. A star companion in the garden, repellant of a wide range of pests above and below the soil.

Preferred Conditions: There are two types of garlic: softneck and hardneck. Softnecks do well in zones 4 to 7; hardnecks prefer cooler zones 1 to 6.

Spacing: 4 to 6 inches (10 to 15 cm) apart.

Planting Method: Prepare the soil so it's nice and loose, then plant individual garlic cloves, upright, 4 to 6 inches (10 to 15 cm) apart. Plant them in late fall, right before your first frost, for a midsummer harvest.

Light: Full sun.

Companion Plants: Brassicas, lettuce, carrots, potatoes, dill, fruit trees.

The Hot Crops—Plants for Summer

I might not be able to be out in the heat of Tennessee for long, but many of my favorite plants thrive in the scorching weather. While the plants bask in the summer sun and absorb the abundance of light, my task is to make sure all of my plants are well watered and nourished. In the peak of summer, I fall into my routine of waking up at dawn before the morning mist has faded and the leaves are dripping dew to make sure my plants are prepared for the day. I was never much of a morning person before gardening, but it's changed my life for the better. In the summer, my days are full and rewarding.

The preferred temperature for the warm season ranges from 75 to 95°F (24 to 35°C). The ideal time to plant would be right after your last risk of frost, or midspring. To not overwhelm yourself when it comes time to harvest, it's beneficial to succession plant your crops to pluck throughout the season rather than all at once. Such crops as tomatoes, peppers and eggplants can transplant very well, so if you want to get a head start on their growth, start them indoors six to eight weeks before your last frost date. This improves your chances of getting bountiful harvests throughout the season, especially if you're in a cooler growing zone. Other crops, such as corn, beans and squash, perform best when directly planted from seed in the soil. Their root system is delicate and they can go into shock if handled too roughly during transplanting. Summer crops are typically very sensitive to the cold. Frosty temperatures can cause quite a bit of damage, so either prepare yourself with a frost blanket or harvest what you can before the cold snap.

Now that you've been briefly introduced to hot crops, let's dive deeper into their preferred growing conditions.

Tomatoes

Now, when I think of abundance, tomatoes always come to mind! They're my all-time favorite plant to grow in the garden. The entire process brings me joy: starting the seed, planting it in the garden, tending to it, smelling the tomato leaves on my fingertips and the unmatched satisfaction of biting into a sun-kissed tomato. A tomato is the happiness of summer perfectly packaged in a juicy, tender fruit.

Preferred Conditions: Grown as an annual in zones 5 to 8. Can grow year-round in zones 9 to 11, depending on the variety. They enjoy deep waterings right to the root, but don't like moisture on their leaves. Consistent pruning of leaves allows for better airflow. Not frost hardy.

Spacing: 18 to 24 inches (45 to 61 cm) apart.

Planting Method: Transplant after your final frost date. The deeper you plant the stem, the stronger of a root system it will create, leading to a happier and healthier plant. Plant in nutrient-rich soil and fertilize throughout the season for consistent productivity.

Light: Full sun.

Companion Plants: Carrots, peppers, cucumbers, beans, onions, radishes, basil, thyme, marigolds, nasturtiums, zinnias.

Tomato Tip! If you tickle the tomato flowers, it can help the flowers pollinate and produce fruit. Both the male and female organs are within a single flower, so shaking them up helps increase their chances of pollinating. Tickle-tickle-tickle.

Peppers

Okay, I lied. When I think about abundance, I'm really talking about peppers! Peppers are, by far, the most productive crops in the garden. I play my part in making sure they're well fed and they reward me with hundreds of crunchy fruits. The flavor profiles range from sweet, mild, hot to nuclear, so double-check the intensity before settling on which varieties to grow.

Preferred Conditions: Grown as an annual in zones 4 to 8. Can grow year-round in zones 9 to 11, depending on the variety. Not frost hardy.

Spacing: 18 inches (45 cm) apart.

Planting Method: Transplant after your final frost date. Plant in nutrient-rich soil and fertilize throughout the season for consistent productivity.

Light: Full sun.

Companion Plants: Carrots, tomatoes, beans, okra, corn, onions, garlic, basil, thyme, dill, marigolds, nasturtiums, zinnias.

Eggplants

Personally, I never enjoyed eggplant much until I started growing it myself and found a world of different varieties! They come in so many different shapes, colors and sizes. Not to mention, the plant itself can be quite the spectacle in the garden. Large, velvety leaves with rich purple stems give a striking display. Some varieties even have thorns, so be mindful when tending to your plants or harvesting. Here in Tennessee, eggplants are very susceptible to pesky flea beetles, so a helpful tip is to plant them in containers high off the ground.

Preferred Conditions: Grown as an annual in zones 4 to 9. Can grow year-round in zones 10 to 11, depending on the variety. Not frost hardy.

Spacing: 18 inches (45 cm) apart.

Planting Method: Transplant after your final frost date. Plant in nutrient-rich soil and fertilize throughout the season for consistent productivity.

Light: Full sun.

Companion Plants: Carrots, peppers, tomatoes, beans, onions, garlic, basil, thyme, dill, marigolds, nasturtiums, zinnias, catnip.

Corn

I feel at peace in the garden when I hear the rustling of cornstalks as they tower over me with a gentle nudge from a passing breeze. Corn is a favorite in the garden, offering a dramatic range of height and colors. This is the tallest of the famous Three Sisters (see page 90). Corn, with her strong and reliable stalk, provides support for searching bean vines and a snug canopy for engorging squashes.

Preferred Conditions: Growing zones 3 to 11, depending on the variety. Corn enjoys frequent waterings so the soil remains moist. Not frost hardy.

Spacing: 8 to 12 inches (20 to 30 cm) apart.

Planting Method: Direct sow after final frost. Succession plant for prolonged harvests. Plant in rich, loamy soil.

Light: Full sun.

Companion Plants: Squash, pumpkins, melons, beans, potatoes, radishes, basil, dill, cosmos, nasturtiums.

Beans

The powerhouse of the garden. Beans can either bush or vine, offering a wider range of placements. They provide an abundance of nutrients to us and their fellow companions. Legumes pull nitrogen from the air and fix it back into the earth through a symbiotic relationship with the soil's microbes. It's what makes them the perfect middle sister in the Three Sisters. They keep the peace between squash and corn by replenishing nutrients throughout the season.

Preferred Conditions: Grown as an annual in zones 2 to 9. Can grow year-round in zones 10 to 11, depending on the variety. Not frost hardy.

Spacing: 2 to 4 inches (5 to 10 cm) apart for bush beans, 4 to 6 inches (10 to 15 cm) apart for pole beans with vertical support.

Planting Method: Soak overnight and direct sow after final frost. Succession plant for prolonged harvests. Plant in well-draining soil.

Light: Full sun.

Companion Plants: Cabbage, cauliflower, kale, lettuce, peppers, tomatoes, eggplants, squash, pumpkins, melons, cucumbers, potatoes, rosemary, basil, marigolds, nasturtiums.

< Fun fact: The strands of hair coming out of corn ears are called silks. Each individual strand is connected to an individual kernel inside the corn husk. For a full ear of corn, make sure you get pollen from the tassels on each silk. You can do so by planting your corn in large groups, enabling more pollen to rain down, or cut a tassel off and brush the silks yourself.

Squashes

The squash family is diverse, to say the least. From its lineage, it provides us with summer and winter squashes, zucchini, melons, gourds and cucumbers.

Summer Squash

Summer squash—moist, tender and soft-skinned—are readily available through the warm season. They grow very quickly, so be sure to check them frequently after planting. Some varieties are viners; others, bush. Regardless of their growth habit, these squashes can become very big. Their large leaves create a striking visual effect while shading the soil underneath. This makes squash the final member of the Three Sisters. Her shade helps retain moisture and keeps everyone refreshed throughout the season as she follows her own path.

Preferred Conditions: Growing zones 3 to 9, depending on the variety. Not frost hardy.

Spacing: 24 to 30 inches (61 to 76 cm) apart.

Planting Method: Direct sow after final frost. Succession plant for prolonged harvests. Plant in rich, loamy soil.

Light: Full sun.

Companion Plants: Radishes, corn, peas, beans, pumpkin, marigolds, nasturtiums.

Winter Squash

Abundant and hardy, the winter squashes grow hard-shelled skin throughout the summer, making them ideal for storage during the colder months. For proper storage, winter squashes need to be cured to enhance their longevity. Winter squash varieties include acorn squash, butternut squash, spaghetti squash and pumpkins. Most winter squashes are viners, so spacing between rows should be at least 6 feet (1.8 m) apart.

Preferred Conditions: Growing zones 3 to 9, depending on the variety. Not frost hardy.

Spacing: 24 to 30 inches (61 to 76 cm) apart.

Planting Method: Direct sow after final frost. Succession plant for prolonged harvests. Plant in rich, loamy soil.

Light: Full sun.

Companion Plants: Radishes, corn, peas, beans, , marigolds, nasturtiums.

Zucchini

The green relative of summer squashes. The main difference between the two is the array of deep green colorings of zucchini. Their elusive emerald skin can make it easy to miss a few during harvests, which pleasantly surprises you in the fall. Zucchini flowers also make a delicious floral snack.

Preferred Conditions: Growing zones 3 to 9, depending on the variety. Not frost hardy.

Spacing: 24 to 30 inches (61 to 76 cm) apart.

Planting Method: Direct sow after final frost. Succession plant for prolonged harvests. Plant in rich, loamy soil.

Companion Plants: Radishes, corn, peas, beans, pumpkin, marigolds, nasturtiums.

Melons

While members of the same family, melons differ greatly because of their tastes and textures. Melons include cantaloupe, honeydew and watermelon. A favorite to grow in the garden for their refreshing rewards on a hot summer day.

Preferred Conditions: Growing zones 4 to 10, depending on the variety. Not frost hardy.

Spacing: 36 to 42 inches (91 to 106 cm) apart.

Planting Method: Direct sow after final frost. Succession plant for prolonged harvests. Plant in rich, loamy soil.

Light: Full sun.

Companion Plants: Radishes, corn, peas, beans, pumpkin, marigolds, nasturtiums.

Cucumbers

A productive and refreshing member of the family. The long, cylindrical fruits provide relief on a warm day out in the garden or a tangy crunch if pickled. Cucumbers are climbers, so give them some vertical support for the best results.

Preferred Conditions: Growing zones 4 to 11, depending on the variety. Not frost hardy.

Spacing: 36 to 42 inches (91 to 106 cm) apart.

Planting Method: Direct sow after final frost. Succession plant for prolonged harvests. Plant in rich, loamy soil.

Light: Full sun.

Companion Plants: Radishes, onions, carrots, corn, peas, beans, pumpkin, marigolds, nasturtiums.

Sweet Potatoes

Sweet potatoes and potatoes may look deceptively similar, but they belong to two completely different families. Potatoes are members of the nightshade family, making them relatives of tomatoes, peppers and eggplants. Stranger yet, sweet potatoes are actually related to morning glories. They produce an abundance of food and vines. Unlike many viners in the garden, sweet potato vines do not tether themselves to support on their own, so they'll need to be trained. If you want to enjoy the bulbous roots, give them plenty of space and loose soil.

Preferred Conditions: Annuals in growing zones 5 to 8. Perennials in growing zones 9 to 11. Not frost hardy.

Spacing: 4 to 6 inches (10 to 15 cm) apart.

Planting Method: Prepare the soil so it's nice and loose, then transplant sweet potato slips after final frost.

Light: Full sun.

Companion Plants: Radishes, onions, carrots, garlic, peas, beans, basil, marigolds, nasturtiums.

The Herbs

Here is a collection of herbs that I've found to be very easy growers in the garden and incredibly versatile in the garden, kitchen, and for natural remedies.

Rosemary

Rosemary is a powerful herb that has been cherished by gardeners, chefs and herbalists for centuries. Known for its fragrant aroma and delicate leaves, rosemary is a versatile herb that can be used for both medicinal and culinary purposes. It makes a wonderful companion plant in the garden as well.

Preferred Conditions: A hardy perennial herb that thrives in warm, sunny climates and can grow in zones 6 to 10. However, with proper care and attention, rosemary can be grown in cooler climates as well.

Planting Method: Transplant or direct sow two weeks before final frost.

Light: Full sun.

Medicinal Properties: Rosemary has a long history of use in traditional medicine. The plant contains a number of active compounds which have shown to have anti-inflammatory and antioxidant properties. Rosemary has also been used to improve memory and cognitive function.

Culinary Uses: Rosemary has a strong, woody flavor and pairs well with such herbs as thyme and oregano. To use rosemary in cooking, simply strip the leaves from the stem and chop them finely. Rosemary is a great addition to marinades, rubs and sauces for meats, such as chicken, lamb and pork. It also pairs well with roasted vegetables, such as potatoes, carrots and squash.

Basil

Basil is a beloved herb that has been used in cooking and medicine. With its distinctive aroma and flavor, basil is a staple in my kitchen.

Preferred Conditions: Basil is an annual herb that is sensitive to cold temperatures. It thrives in warm, sunny climates and is commonly grown in zones 2 to 11. Make sure this herb is well watered.

Planting Method: Transplant or direct sow two weeks after final frost.

Light: Full sun.

Medicinal Properties: Basil has anti-inflammatory and antioxidant properties and is also believed to have antibacterial and antiviral properties. Basil has been used to treat a variety of conditions, including coughs, colds and digestive issues. It can also be used topically to soothe insect bites and skin irritations.

Culinary Uses: Basil is commonly used to flavor such dishes as pasta, pizza and salads, especially if they include tomato. The herb has a sweet, peppery flavor and pairs well with such herbs as oregano and thyme. To use basil in cooking, simply strip the leaves from the stem and chop them finely. Basil is a great addition to sauces, soups and marinades. Personally, my favorite way to use basil is to make pesto with sunflower seeds, Parmesan cheese and olive oil.

Green Sage

Green sage, also known as garden sage, is a versatile herb known for its fragrant, velvety leaves and medicinal properties.

Preferred Conditions: Sage is a hardy perennial herb that can be grown in zones 4 to 10.

Planting Method: Transplant two weeks before final frost.

Light: Full sun.

Medicinal Properties: Green sage has anti-inflammatory and antioxidant properties and is also believed to have antibacterial properties. Green sage has been used to treat a variety of conditions, including digestive issues, sore throats and respiratory infections. It has also been used topically or in salves to soothe skin irritations and reduce inflammation.

Culinary Uses: Green sage can be used in such dishes as stuffing, roasted meats and sauces. The herb has a strong, slightly bitter flavor and pairs well with such herbs as thyme and rosemary.

To use green sage in cooking, simply strip the leaves from the stem and chop them finely. Green sage is a great addition to soups, stews and marinades, and to make flavored butter or infused oils.

Lavender

Lavender is a beautiful and fragrant herb that has been cherished for centuries. Its delicate purple flowers and soothing scent make it a popular choice for gardeners, herbalists and aromatherapists.

Preferred Conditions: Lavender is a hardy perennial herb that thrives in warm, sunny climates and is commonly grown in zones 5 to 9. When planting lavender, the soil should be well drained. If your soil is heavy or claylike, consider amending it with sand or perlite to improve drainage.

Planting Method: Transplant two weeks before final frost.

Light: Full sun.

Medicinal Properties: Lavender has a long history of use in traditional medicine. Lavender essential oil is commonly used in aromatherapy to promote relaxation and reduce stress. Lavender has also been used to treat a variety of conditions, including anxiety, insomnia and digestive issues. It has anti-inflammatory and antioxidant properties, and can be used topically to soothe skin irritations and burns.

Culinary Uses: Lavender has a light, sweet and floral flavor and pairs well with such herbs as thyme and rosemary. To use lavender in cooking, simply strip the flowers from the stem and chop them finely. Lavender is a great addition to baked goods and can also be used to flavor teas.

Oregano

Ah, oregano—one of my favorite herbs! Oregano is a versatile and flavorful herb used in a lot of Latin cuisine. It is a member of the mint family and is known for its strong aroma and flavor.

Preferred Conditions: Oregano is a hardy herb that can be grown in zones 4 to 9. I would recommend planting oregano where it will have a lot of space, or in containers, because this herb can and will take over.

Planting Method: Transplant or direct sow two weeks before final frost.

Light: Full sun.

Medicinal Properties: Oregano has long been used for its medicinal properties. It is rich in antioxidants and has been shown to have anti-inflammatory and antimicrobial properties. Oregano tea is commonly used to soothe sore throats and to help with digestion. Oregano oil is also a popular natural remedy for treating colds, flu and other respiratory infections.

Culinary Uses: Oregano is a staple herb in the kitchen and is commonly used in such dishes as pizza and pasta sauce. It pairs well with such herbs as basil and thyme. Oregano can also be used to make flavored vinegars and oils and can be added to marinades for meats and vegetables.

Mint

By far one of the easiest herbs to grow, mint is a versatile and aromatic plant that is loved for its fresh and refreshing flavor.

Preferred Conditions: Mint can be grown in hardiness zones 3 to 11. It prefers cool and moist soil conditions, but can tolerate a wide range of temperatures. I only recommend growing mint in containers because it will easily overrun a space if planted in the ground or among other plants. It can grow wild and easily choke out other plants.

Planting Method: Transplant or direct sow two weeks before final frost.

Light: Full sun or part shade.

Medicinal Properties: Mint is known for its soothing properties and is commonly used to alleviate digestive issues, such as bloating, nausea or gas. Mint tea is also a popular remedy for sore throats and colds, as it has a cooling and soothing effect.

Culinary Uses: Mint is commonly used in such dishes as chutneys, curries and sauces. Mint also pairs well with such herbs as basil, thyme and rosemary and can be used to make flavored vinegars and oils. Mint leaves are a perfect addition to iced teas, lemonades and cocktails on a hot summer day.

Chamomile

Chamomile is a delicate and fragrant herb that is best known for its calming properties. I especially love harvesting its abundant little white flowers.

Preferred Conditions: German chamomile is an annual herb that can be grown in hardiness zones 4 to 9, while Roman chamomile is a perennial that can be grown in zones 4 to 9. Both varieties prefer cooler temperatures and can tolerate light frost.

Planting Method: Transplant or direct sow two weeks before final frost.

Light: Full sun to part shade.

Medicinal Properties: Chamomile is known for its calming and anti-inflammatory properties. It is commonly used to treat anxiety, insomnia and such digestive issues as bloating and indigestion. Chamomile tea is a popular remedy for insomnia as well.

Culinary Uses: Chamomile has a sweet and floral flavor and is often used in herbal teas, desserts and savory dishes. German chamomile is more commonly used for culinary purposes than Roman chamomile is. Chamomile tea can also be used as a natural remedy for such skin conditions as eczema and psoriasis when applied topically. The essential oil of chamomile can also be used in aromatherapy to promote relaxation and reduce stress.

Thyme

What a wonderful herb! In the garden, hardy and low-maintenance thyme can add texture and fragrance to any landscape. It attracts beneficial insects, such as bees and butterflies, and its small, delicate flowers provide a beautiful pop of color.

Preferred Conditions: Thyme is a perennial herb that is hardy in zones 4 to 9. Thyme is a great plant for container gardens, but it also does well in garden beds or rock gardens.

Planting Method: Transplant or direct sow two weeks before final frost.

Light: Full sun.

Medicinal Properties: Thyme has been used to treat respiratory and digestive issues, as well as for its antifungal and antibacterial properties. It can be used fresh or dried, and is often steeped in hot water to make a soothing tea.

Culinary Uses: Thyme is also a popular culinary herb and is often used in Mediterranean and French cuisine. It pairs well with meats, vegetables and even desserts, and its earthy, aromatic flavor can enhance a wide variety of dishes. One of my personal favorite varieties to grow for the kitchen is lemon thyme.

Dill

Dill is a versatile herb with culinary and medicinal uses. Its unique flavor adds a distinct taste to various dishes, making it a popular choice for cooks around the world.

Preferred Conditions: Dill is an annual herb that can be grown in hardiness zones 2 to 11.

Planting Method: Direct sow two weeks before final frost.

Light: Full sun.

Medicinal Properties: Dill has been used for centuries for its medicinal properties. It is known to aid digestion, relieve gas and bloating, and can even help reduce menstrual cramps. Dill is also a natural antimicrobial and can help fight off harmful bacteria.

Culinary Uses: I love dill in the kitchen! Dill has a distinct flavor that is often described as tangy and fresh. It is commonly used in pickling, as well as in salads, dressings and sauces. I love to prepare my own home-made ranch dressing with dill fresh from the garden. Store-bought ranch doesn't even compare.

Chapter 11

Planting Trees

Oh, trees. The gentle giants of the world that tower over us, providing shade and radiating comfort. Their presence in a garden or around your home brings a strong sense of safety with their hypnotic dances as their many leaves blow in the wind. Introducing a tree is not just putting a sapling in the ground, it is an act of love, a connection to the Earth and a commitment to the future. Each tree carries a story of the past, becoming pillars of our ancestors' legacy. Trees are also observers of the story yet to be written, keeping an archive of memories in the rings of their trunk as they watch over the generations that live under their shade. The wise words of the Bengali philosopher Rabindranath Tagore capture their humbling significance: *"The one who plants trees, knowing that he will never sit in their shade, has at least started to understand the meaning of life."* Planting a tree is more than bringing something beautiful to your space—it's also about intentionally leaving behind a legacy for future generations to come.

With so many varieties and their abilities to grow different sized leaves, different colored flowers and different-tasting fruit, it can be challenging deciding which one is the best fit for you. When choosing a tree, think about the soil, the sun and the space available. Will your tree need full sun or partial shade? What type of soil do you have? Is the tree you want to plant going to grow too big for your space? You must first understand your conditions; only then will you begin to know what trees would be best for you and also which trees would be happiest in your space.

Another thing to consider is the influence your tree will have in the garden. Trees cast shade and attract a lot of wildlife. It's important to not only think of the beauty it'll add to your garden or lawn but also the *function* it will serve. It'll create a new environment under its leaves, cooling the earth and blocking the harsh rays of the sun. Suddenly there is room for a shade garden, depending on the size of the tree of course. There are also new birds visiting your land to find refuge on the tree's branches. Those trees play a role in feeding and sheltering them now. How can you use the birds to your advantage? Got a pest issue? Maybe a feathered friend can help.

Trees are influential, but it may not always be positive. Some species of trees can also be very opportunistic, taking full advantage of foreign land and resources while outcompeting the natives. This can threaten the native species of trees and the wide network of wildlife that they support, above and below the soil. I always urge those seeking to plant trees to opt for native species. They'll be much easier to establish because they're accustomed to the local conditions, such as the weather or soil. Native species can also support local wildlife by providing habitat and essential food supply.

When you have found the perfect tree, it is time to plant. Allow me to walk you through the steps and what to think about when it's time for planting.

- Before planting, make sure you have a clear understanding of the type of light, soil and space your desired tree requires and choose a spot that can meet all of those needs.

- When it's time to break ground, dig a hole in the soil that is twice as wide as the root ball and just deep enough so that the top of the root ball sits slightly above the soil line. This will ensure that the roots can breathe and that water does not collect around the base of the tree, which can cause rot.

- Before placing the tree in the hole, make sure to loosen the roots and remove any damaged or broken ones. If your tree came with a burlap or wire basket, cut away any excess material that could impede root growth. Then, gently place the tree in the hole and fill the remaining space with soil and fresh compost, pressing firmly to remove any air pockets.

- Water your tree deeply, making sure the soil is evenly moist but not saturated. A good rule of thumb is to water your tree twice a week for the first month, and then once a week for the first year. You can also add a layer of mulch around the base of the tree, which will help retain moisture, prevent weed growth and protect the ecology of the soil that is developing around the tree.

< A Tennessee native Dogwood in bloom.

- As your tree grows, remember to prune it regularly to encourage healthy growth and remove any damaged or diseased branches. You can also add fertilizer to the soil once a year to help boost growth and maintain the tree's health.

- Take a moment to appreciate the beauty and power of the tree you have planted. As it grows and flourishes, it will provide shade, clean the air and give back to the Earth in ways that are both practical and spiritual. By planting a tree, you are creating a legacy that will last for generations to come. Over time, it will feel like your tree has become a part of the family, growing with you through the rain and shine.

Trees are guardians of the planet. They have the invaluable power to sequester carbon, cool the climate and clean the air, making them essential to the health and well-being of our planet.

Through photosynthesis, trees absorb carbon dioxide from the atmosphere and convert it into organic matter. The carbon they pull from the atmosphere is stored in the tree's trunk, branches and leaves, making them a carbon bank. In fact, a mature tree can sequester up to 48 pounds (22 kg) of carbon dioxide per year, making it an incredibly effective tool for mitigating the effects of climate change. And whatever they do not store within their trunks, they seep through their roots to be stored in the soil. I want you to understand that planting trees is quite literally one of the greatest things we can do to combat the growing reserve of carbon in the atmosphere. When you plant a tree, you're making a major contribution.

But that's not all. Trees also have the power to cool the climate. Through a process known as *evapotranspiration*, trees release water vapor into the atmosphere, which helps cool the surrounding air. In fact, just one mature tree can have the cooling effect of 10 air-conditioning units. And of course, the shade that they cast cools the Earth and all those seeking refuge from the intensity of the sun.

And if that wasn't enough, trees also play a critical role in cleaning the air we breathe. Through their leaves, trees absorb such pollutants as nitrogen dioxide, sulfur dioxide and ozone, as well as microscopic particles like dust and smoke. In exchange for all of these compounds, they release oxygen, the chemical element necessary for our survival.

Planting a tree reminds us that we are part of something bigger than ourselves, that we are connected to every living being on this planet. They offer us a sense of grounding, of rootedness and of belonging. And in doing so, they remind us of our responsibility to care for and protect the Earth that sustains us.

Chapter 12
Garden Maintenance

The garden teaches us many things, but one of the greatest things we learn from it is how to properly tend to our own needs. While gardening is an incredibly joyous experience, it comes with a lot of responsibility. To commit to a garden is to commit to the labor of love it needs for it to thrive. As I was learning the way of tending to the many plants in my garden, I couldn't help but notice the way it mirrored how we're meant to tend to ourselves. It's funny really; I'm not sure what's more challenging to face: the amount of work it takes to care for a garden or the parts of ourselves that we're hesitant to overcome to be able to grow.

A moment of myself walking through the garden, gently holding the leaf of corn as I walk past.

Being Present in the Garden

Time. The unseeable force that carries us forward. You blink and suddenly years have passed. In this digital era with distractions bombarding us at every turn, it's easy to lose track of how precious every second really is. I can't think of a greater demonstration of time's importance than the garden. In the cold months of winter, as snow covers the yard, it can feel as though time has gone still. Then suddenly, the snow melts, the air warms and, like clockwork, plants know the exact moment to rise. With the inevitability of winter, they know time is of the essence.

Within the constraint of the seasons, they must successfully grow, bloom and reproduce. There's not a moment to lose; every second counts.

When we commit to the garden, we must commit the time necessary not only to tend it, but to observe it as well. Every day, every minute is a chance to witness the wonders that play out among all the abundance. A seed sprouting, true leaves forming, flowers blooming, butterflies hatching, birds singing, the sun setting.

We must be present in the garden both with our time and our attention. As it pertains to maintaining the garden, it's important to check on your plants often so you can build a relationship with them. You learn to look out for signs of struggle, such as wilting leaves or a chewed stem. The larger the garden, the more time it will take to check on everything, so if you don't necessarily have the time to care for a larger space, start small and work your way up to what you know you can manage with the amount of time you have to give.

The more time we spend with our gardens, the more tapped in we become to their rhythm. The more time we are able to spend paying attention to our plants, the more we realize what we need to do to take care of them. We begin to hone in on the natural cycle happening all around us. When the redbuds bloom, it's time to sow seeds; when the oak's leaves start coming in, it's time for a next wave of plants to be sown; when the goldenrods bloom, it's

almost time to harvest. We learn the timing of things by noticing the connections being made right before our eyes. The signs happen all around us; we just have to get out of our own heads and pay attention.

As I learned about being present in the garden, it reflected our need to be present with ourselves and listen to our feelings. The way external forces can influence the garden, they can influence us, too. It's important to give ourselves the time we need to attend to how we're being affected by life and the experiences it brings. Only with the awareness of what is happening within us and within our gardens can we take the actions necessary to make any changes to continue growing.

Time is precious. I can't imagine spending it with words left unsaid, feelings unexpressed and dreams unpursued. The greatest gift we have in this life is time; let's use it to live a life we actually love.

Watering

Something important to understand is that, when we introduce plants to our garden, they come with their own set of needs that must be met so they can grow to their fullest potential. Plants native to your area have adapted to the conditions of their environment, so they thrive in the region's climate. One of the greatest adaptations is their differing reliance on water. This can vary greatly from plant to plant, depending on what they've adapted to in their native environment. Plants found by the river or in bogs would need consistent and heavy moisture to thrive, because that's what they've evolved to exist in. Meanwhile, desert plants have evolved to live on very little available moisture.

Every plant has a different desire for water, so it's important to have a clear understanding of what the plants you're introducing will need. I'm frequently asked when plants should be watered and I frequently reply that it depends on the plant. This is why I recommend that beginners start off by hand watering the garden to build the relationship with water throughout your garden. Irrigation can be immensely valuable if you don't have the time or patience to hand water, but I feel that you lose the opportunity to really be present with each of your plants. I love being the hand that nourishes my garden. Some plants won't need to be watered every day, but others may appreciate it. Some external conditions will also influence how often and how much you need to water. For example, if you're in an area where it rains often, naturally you needn't water as much. In fact, you may have to find ways to prevent overwatering of certain plants. Those conditions would differ greatly from someone in a drier climate, who will need to water more frequently. The best thing you can do to understand when to water is to become a master of your own unique environmental conditions.

Another tip when it comes to watering is that it's ideal to do it earlier in the morning, before the intensity of the sun is at its peak. When watering, aim directly for the roots and avoid watering over the leaves, especially if you're caught watering in the middle of the day. The reason is the water droplets that form can actually act as a magnifying glass on the leaves, refracting the intense rays of the sun, which can lead to scorching on the leaves. Some plants like tomatoes can also develop diseases if there's too much moisture building up on the leaves. Get your hose right to the base of the stem and water directly into the roots.

Even though gardening has become a core practice in my life, I still haven't managed to become a morning person. The early hours right before the sun peeks over the horizon are a special time in the garden. You hear the calls from the birds letting the others know they made it through the night and you feel the morning dew that has built up on the leaves splash your feet. Those few precious hours, a magical time to be in the garden, are the best time to water your plants and start the day off in a state of bliss.

A great way to really extend the impact of your watering is to *mulch* your garden beds. Mulch is a layer of material that is spread over the soil surface in a garden or landscape. It can be made up of a variety of materials such as leaves, grass clippings, straw, wood chips, bark, or compost.

The garden teaches us the importance of being watered. Plants show us firsthand how abundantly they grow when their needs are met. Some thrive on little, while others prefer to live in ponds. Like plants, people also vary as to whatever water may symbolize in their lives. To me, water reflects our need for joy in life. To water ourselves means to take the time to do things that bring us joy. We live in a society where we're conditioned to give so much of ourselves to everyone around us. While I believe it is important to give to our communities and our loved ones, there's only so much we can give before we pour out the last drops from our cup. There comes a time when we must know to stop and give back to ourselves. Do something just for you. Something that brings you immense joy or even just rest. We cannot pour from an empty glass, so fill it up!

A gentle watering of a pepper plant.

Weeding

Personally, I don't like the term *weeding*. It makes it sound like the plants around us are a nuisance, when in reality, they hold some incredible benefits. Many wild plants that tend to try to establish themselves in our garden beds may actually be edible and could even hold medicinal properties, so be sure to research them before you pull them out. Rather than "weeding," it can be thought of as "harvesting." When you shift your perspective from *weed* to *food* or *herb*, you suddenly awaken to the incredible abundance that Mother Nature already provides to us.

The reason it's recommended to *harvest* these opportunistic plants is that, at the end of the day, they also require nutrients, water and space to thrive. These are precious resources in a garden that can hinder the

Often considered a "weed," lamb's quarters are actually purifying plants that help restore healthy nutrients to poor quality soil. This unique plant is also edible and very nutritious.

growth of the plants you're trying to cultivate. If you make your own compost, it's common for the seeds of broken-down fruits to make their way into the mix and you'll find them sprouting in your beds. If it's not something you planned for, these other plants can become a problem in the future. Sometimes, I like to pot some of those volunteers and allow them to live elsewhere; it'd be a shame to pass up the extra abundance.

When removing any unwanted plants, I tend to lean toward the old-fashioned plucking of smaller seedlings. If they've grown to larger size, I either use pruners to snip the base of the plant off the root or pull it out meticulously, trying to disturb the soil as little as possible. Sometimes, I try to pluck and I end up snapping the leaves right off the base. The thing about a lot of these native plants is that they're tough. They can easily grow right back from that remaining root system, so it's best to remove it completely.

I implore you to never use any chemicals to deal with weeds, especially around a food garden. Persistent toxins can cause a lot of damage to the ecology of the soil that can take many years to recover from. I'd also be wary of consuming anything grown with such abrasive chemicals around, be it in the ground, on the plants or in the air.

Like the garden, there can be things that latch on to us, such as limiting beliefs, unhealthy relationships or trauma. The longer we allow these things to fester within our lives, the deeper their roots seep in, slowly sucking away more and more of our energy. We may snap away what's at the surface, but the deeper root remains. Sometimes, you need to take things from the source and slowly pull them out. It will take patience and work, but the relief you will feel when you've been released from its clutches will be worth it. By doing so, we create more space for growth.

Pruning

Pruning is an essential practice in gardening, as it helps shape and direct the growth of plants, encouraging them to reach their fullest potential. Just as how each plant has its unique water needs, each plant also has its unique pruning needs, depending on the species and desired shape. Pruning can help improve the overall health of the plant by removing diseased or damaged branches, promoting air circulation and stimulating new growth.

A great example would be tomatoes. There are tomato varieties that are considered indeterminate tomatoes, sometimes referred to as "vining" tomatoes. They produce fruit continuously throughout the growing season, until the first frost. Because of this, indeterminate tomatoes require more main-tenance, such as staking or trellising, to keep the plant upright and the fruit off the ground. In the case of indeterminate tomatoes, it's extremely beneficial to prune off new arms to redirect energy back into fruit produc-tion, otherwise the new arms can take over and hinder the current ripening fruit from growing to its fullest potential.

Determinate tomatoes are sometimes referred to as "bush" tomatoes. These plants tend to grow to a certain height, usually around 2 to 3 feet (61 to 91 cm), and then stop growing. They also tend to produce all their fruit at once, over a period of a few weeks.

Once the fruit has ripened, the plant will start to die back, meaning leaves will begin to brown and it reaches the end of its life cycle. In the case of the determinate variety, because the plant can get quite bushy, it would be very beneficial to prune any overlapping branches or leaves, to promote air circulation and reduce the chance of a common disease known as *blight*, which occurs from a lack of air flow and buildup of moisture on the leaves.

Just as plants need pruning to reach their fullest potential, humans could also use a good clearing of old energy. This pruning can involve letting go of things that no longer serve us, such as unhealthy relationships or negative thought patterns, and cultivating new habits and behaviors that align with our values and goals. "Pruning" can help us lead more fulfilling and purposeful lives, just as it helps plants grow and flourish.

However, just as with pruning plants, pruning in our lives can be painful and difficult. It may involve letting go of things that we are attached to, or facing difficult truths about ourselves. But just as the pain of pruning plants leads to healthier growth, the pain of pruning in our lives can ultimately lead to greater happiness and fulfillment. By regu-larly assessing and pruning our lives, we can become the best versions of ourselves and live the life we truly desire.

Fertilizing

As a gardener, I have come to understand the importance of nourishing my plants with the right nutrients. Just like humans, plants need a balanced diet to grow healthy and strong. While soil can provide some nutrients, it's not always enough, especially for plants that are heavy feeders. This is where fertilizing comes in.

When I transplant anything into the garden, I like to add a scoop or two of plant food, made up of 10 parts compost, 4 parts organic vegetable fertilizer, 2 parts bone meal and 1 part Epsom salts. Plants need different nutrients for different functions. Fruiting plants require more potassium and phosphate to produce their abundance of fruit, and that's why I add the vegetable fertilizer. This, along with the compost, also provides essential nitrogen, which is necessary for their green growth, the growth of their stems and leaves. I add bone meal to give an added boost of calcium, which fortifies the plants' root system for tougher plants overall. Lastly, I sprinkle in pure Epsom salts to add a boost of magnesium, which helps plants properly absorb and store the other necessary nutrients.

I add this mix at the initial planting, but once my plants begin to produce fruit, I get on a biweekly fertilizing schedule to continue supplementing them with all the necessary nutrients. I supplement with a special fertilizing tea I make out of comfrey, which makes for a potassium-rich concoction. See page 74 for how I make my comfrey tea.

When fertilizing, I always dilute the mixture with 10 parts water to 1 part comfrey tea, because it is so powerful. I fill up my watering can and pour the blend directly into the root system of my plants. One more tip is that I usually like to fertilize when my plants are on the drier side, because they'll be more receptive to the water with the added nutrients.

Something I've observed with fertilizing as well is to be cautious not to overload your plants, either. Overfertilizing can harm plants, especially when using synthetic fertilizers. It's far less common when using all natural and organic, so I always recommend going with those options. Not to mention, synthetic fertilizers take a much longer time to break down in the soil so they can actually suffocate and kill off the vital microbes. Ultimately, it comes down to giving your plants a sustainable and balanced diet of nutrients.

In the way different plants need different types of fertilizers, there are also many different ways to nourish ourselves as humans. Some people may find nourishment through spending time in Nature, others through spending time with loved ones, still others through meditation or prayer. What's most important is discovering what works best for you. What works for one may not necessarily work for another, so do not be afraid to experiment and search for things outside of your comfort zone. You may be pleasantly surprised by what you find.

Harvesting

Something that many beginner gardeners often overlook is the importance of harvesting from their garden regularly. When you have a thriving garden, it's easy to get caught up in the excitement of watching it grow and forget to harvest the fruits of your labor.

Plants are designed to produce fruits and vegetables for a reason. When the fruit is ripe, it contains all the nutrients and energy that the plant has stored up during its growth. If you don't harvest the fruit in a timely manner, the plant will eventually stop producing altogether. Not only that, but leaving overripe fruits on the plant can also attract pests and diseases that could harm your garden. If I'm being honest, sometimes I hesitate to harvest because the plants just look so full and beautiful. However, harvesting is a crucial part of keeping your garden healthy and productive.

When I started my garden, I was so excited to get things in the ground, I just went ahead and fully planted all of my beds. As the season progressed, I quickly realized how overwhelming it was to have to harvest everything so close together. There was just so much abundance! I ended up not being able to harvest everything in time and some plants bolted; others had fruits that rotted; and some things I forgot about altogether. It was a pleasant surprise while preparing the beds, next season, to find left-behind carrots. The following season, to help break up the times to harvest, I practiced succession planting, which simply means to space out the times at which you plant. This allows for smaller waves of plants reaching maturity at once, which makes harvesting a lot less overwhelming. It's still hard to contain my excitement when it's time to plant, but it's better for you and the garden in the long run.

Just like plants, we are meant to grow and flourish, producing fruits that can benefit others around us. If we don't take action to harvest our own potential, we can become stagnant and lead unfulfilling lives. You owe it to yourself to live a fruitful life. It can be scary to reach for the life you know you deserve, but it's worth it. It's never too late to realize your potential. Just like plants, everyone has their own timing. Go ahead and harvest from your garden, and don't forget to take the time to harvest the potential within yourself when you're ready.

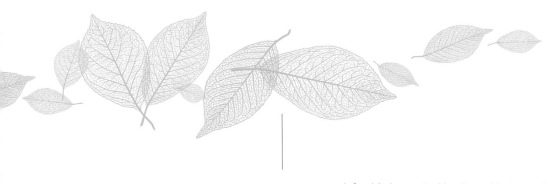

A freshly harvested basket of fruits and veggies.>

Pest Management through Plants

The most common question I get asked from beginners is how to get rid of bugs in the garden. With a deep sigh and smile, I always let them know that bugs are actually essential to a garden. If anything, we should invite them in rather than being so focused on pushing them out. I do so by planting a wide diversity of plants in my garden so as to create a thriving ecosystem. When we do so, every plant that is introduced to the garden invites its own unique set of birds, critters, insects, spiders and microbes.

When we limit ourselves to a select few plants, we leave our garden vulnerable to pests because there isn't a web of other creatures to help manage them. You see, bugs are our *friends*. By planting a variety of plants, we create a more resilient and diverse ecosystem that can better withstand pests, diseases and environmental stressors. For example, planting certain flowers can attract beneficial insects, such as ladybugs, lacewings and parasitic wasps that feed on pests like aphids and cabbage worms. In turn, these beneficial insects can help control pest populations and reduce the need for pesticides altogether.

I strongly urge gardeners to never spray toxic chemicals in the garden to manage pests, for a few reasons. First, when you spray chemicals to target a specific pest, whatever you're spraying will affect every living thing around it, not just the creature you're after. That can cause devastating effects to the precious ecosystem you're trying so hard to cultivate. Second, even worse, as it rains, those chemicals will eventually leach into the soil and wreak havoc on the delicate network of life underground, which can take many years to recover. Lastly, those toxic chemicals are persistent and take incredible lengths of time to break down. As rain continues to fall, it drains through the soil and carries those toxic chemicals with it until it reaches an underground stream, where it then feeds into our creeks, rivers, lakes and oceans. Toxic chemicals may not only cause the plants to become toxic to eat, but introduce harmful substances to the air we breathe in our garden or through our windows. The consequences are monumental and it can all be avoided with a simple solution. Plant more plants!

Plants can also help you build better soil. Different plants have different root structures and nutrient requirements, which can help improve soil health and prevent soil erosion. Plants also release different compounds into the soil, some of which can help suppress diseases or attract beneficial microbes that aid in plant growth. Truly, whenever you have a problem in the garden, there is a plant that can help!

Remember: Every plant has its unique and vital contribution to the ecosystem. Aim to plant a wide mix of native flowers, vegetables, herbs and fruits. By doing so, we can create a garden that not only provides us with delicious food and beautiful flowers but also supports a thriving ecosystem and encourages native wildlife.

Like our gardens, humans also thrive when we embrace diversity. When we limit ourselves to a select few ideas, beliefs or opinions, we leave ourselves vulnerable to ignorance and intolerance. By embracing diversity in all its forms, we can create a more balanced and harmonious world. Just like in the garden, each individual has their unique contribution to the world, and by working together, we can create a society that supports and uplifts every member. *Nature teaches us that diversity is necessary.*

The largest cabbage I've ever grown. You'll noticed it's full of holes and bitten leaves. This is what organic gardening can look like. Plants are very resilient; a few bite marks will not alter the quality of your crops. I'd rather have cabbage with holes in it than use toxic chemicals. When companion planting, do not expect every pest to disappear; they will most certainly still be there, but you'll have the help of predatory insects to help manage pest populations.

A perennial border of flowers in the vegetable garden.

Chapter 13

The Changing of Seasons

Preparing for a New Season

As the winter months come to an end and the first signs of spring begin to appear, it's time to start thinking about preparing your garden for a new growing season. I like to get out there as soon as the soil is workable. By taking the time to prepare your garden properly, you can help ensure a successful and bountiful harvest. Here are the steps you should follow to prepare your garden for a new growing season:

- Before you can begin planting, you need to clear your garden of any debris and weeds that may have accumulated over the winter months. To help build the soil ecology, I recommend cutting or sawing off any dead plants at the base and leaving the root system intact to break down in the soil. I also leave any decayed stems or foliage in the soil as well. I even leave the mulch from last season in place. The more plant material in the ground, the better. All of the remaining plant debris will be covered in the next step. Similarly, if a weed has a shallow root system, I cut it off at the base rather than pull it, to disturb the soil as little as possible. As it breaks down, it just becomes more sustenance for the garden. If a weed has a deeper taproot, then I pull to ensure it doesn't continue to come back.

- The quality of your soil is crucial to the success of your garden, so it's important to amend it properly. Add a 3-inch (7.5-cm) layer of organic matter, such as compost, well-rotted manure or worm castings, to your soil. This will help improve soil structure and provide essential nutrients for your plants.

- After amending the soil, add a 3-inch (7.5-cm) layer of mulch to help suppress weeds and retain moisture throughout the season. I like to add my mulch before planting because I find it easier to move the mulch to plant than to lay mulch down around already planted plants. It's less time consuming being able to spread the mulch out evenly without obstacles.

- With your soil prepared, you're ready for the season and you can start planting!

The End of the Season

As the growing season comes to an end and the leaves begin to change color, it's time to prepare your garden for the winter or to fallow, meaning to take a season to rest. By doing so, you can help improve the health and productivity of your soil, and ensure that your garden is ready to thrive when the next growing season arrives.

- The very first thing you'll want to do is harvest all your remaining crops, especially before any frost creeps in and spoils your fruits. I always find it bittersweet to have my final harvest. I'm excited to rest, but I'll miss the daily harvests.

- This is a bonus step to those who have such birds as chickens, ducks or quail. An amazing benefit to having chickens is they can be your cleanup crew at the end of the season. I release the ladies into the garden to peck and scratch away at the remaining plants and beds. The chickens help clean up the garden, covering the beds in plant debris to break down into the soil, naturally loosening up the mulch and soil and feeding the soil with their manure as they scavenge and poop. By the time the chickens have had their fun, you have a clean slate for the new year.

- The remaining stalks, stems, branches and leaves are all left intact in the garden over the winter to provide shelter and refuge to wildlife through the cold months. It can all be cut back in the spring.

- If you plan to leave your garden fallow for a season, consider planting a cover crop. Cover crops, such as clover, rye or vetch, can help improve soil health, prevent erosion and provide essential nutrients for your soil. Plant your cover crops according to the instructions on the seed packets and be sure to water them regularly. When the next growing season arrives, you can apply the no-till method over the cover crop to improve soil fertility.

I allow nature to run its course in my garden through the winter and leave the amending for the spring.

The vegetable garden at sunset

Winter: A Time of Rest and Reflection

I grew up in the bone-chilling streets of Chicago, where the howling winds of winter could pierce right through you. I dreaded the end of autumn because I knew of the suffering to come. I never would have imagined that one day I'd become grateful for the cold, but here I am.

A few lifetimes later, and I am now in the shoes of a gardener. I'm grateful to be living the life I do in the countryside of Tennessee, but gardening is truly a labor of love. Heavy on the labor. By mid-March, I am out in the gardens planting the first round of cool crops that were actually started indoors two months prior. The season lasts until mid-November, and by the end of it, I am drained, never wanting to see a pair of pruning shears or smell tomato leaves ever again. By the time winter hits, I am ready for the rest that comes with it.

Younger me would be shocked to hear that I've learned to appreciate the cold. Besides the relief that comes with being able to physically rest my body from an abundant growing season, I've come to an understanding of just how important rest is in every aspect of life. Our external environment isn't the only place in our lives where we experience a winter. Our spirit, our relationships, our emotions and our work all go through their waves of cool. A stillness. What feels like a low so low, you can't even muster the strength to leave your bed.

Well, Nature has taught that winters are not just okay, they are necessary. So necessary, in fact, that there are plants that would malfunction without a cold plunge. These plants begin to lose their leaves in autumn, preparing to go dormant as their brown petals make for the Earth. As winter creeps in, they're nothing more than skeletons of their former selves, giving the illusion of death. While it may look like there isn't much going on aboveground, the network below is still at work, roots expanding, depths deepening and foundations strengthening. Once the snow begins to melt and the days get warmer, they prepare for rebirth with new buds forming and the first signs of new growth emerging. In spring, they begin to stretch toward the sky, as if experiencing the bliss of pandiculation after months asleep. They're stronger than ever before, and before you know it, they're putting on their most colorful display of flowers. The most glorious bloom you've ever seen. The cycle to winter repeats again. The petals begin to wilt as the seed heads engorge. By fall, the plant is browning, ready for rest after a year of successful reproduction.

Just like plants, we must allow ourselves to undergo these winters. And we must allow ourselves to rest free from the guilt of not working that we've been indoctrinated with. *Resting is productive.* While it may look like not much is happening on the surface, healing, restoration and growth are happening within. Once we've taken the time to rest, we're ready to reach, grow and bloom brighter than before.

Pedaling back to the work in the garden, winter is also the time to reflect on your growing season. Did everything go as planned? What would you do differently? What incredible natural moments did you witness? What did you learn? Take all the lessons and prepare for a new year of abundance, after your much needed rest, of course.

Conclusion: Mastering Your Conditions

I hope that you take the insight shared through these pages and integrate it into your practices in the garden and your life. As much as I can share about my own garden, what I want you to understand is that no two gardens are the same. They each face their own unique set of conditions, such as the weather, soil, climate or gardener. The variables vary greatly, but one truth ripples through them all: Everyone has the potential to grow a garden.

To grow a garden, you must become a master of your conditions so that you can know how to provide everything that your plants need to thrive under those conditions. The fundamental needs of plants are universal. Every plant needs, to some degree, a certain amount of moisture, nutrition, space, light, maintenance and type of soil. The amount that those plants will need will vary from plant to plant, and the way one gardener in one region meets those needs will differ from how someone in a different region will meet those conditions, too.

To truly get the most out of your garden, you should paint a clear picture in your mind of what you want and set the intention to go for it. Take a deep breath, close your eyes and really visualize the abundance of your garden. The scent of flowers, the brushing of the leaves on your skin, the smooth surface of fresh fruits. Picture it all in your mind's eye and claim it. It is yours. The journey to a life of abundance awaits you. Grab your straw hat, strap on your boots and begin your journey back to the soil.

As in our gardens, we must become a master of our own unique set of conditions. Every single one of us has our own unique story and we must become the master of the narrative. We are each dealt our own set of cards and we must learn how to best play our hand. I know I've given you a lot to think about throughout this guide. All I hope is that I've been able to provide you with the tools and inspiration to get out there to create a garden and life full of abundance.

Acknowledgments

I owe a great deal of my success to my beloved partner, Domonick Gravine, for his patience, his tenacity and his guidance through the magnificent world of gardening. I'm immensely grateful for all that he has shown me and I'm honored to be cultivating this magical place with him.

I can't go without expressing the immense gratitude I feel for my community on social media. The reciprocation of our love for this world and the abundance it brings has brought me more inspiration and drive than they could ever know. We have learned together and we have grown together. I cannot wait to see all that we accomplish together.

I must acknowledge and thank the sacred piece of land that I am on, the trees that have shared their wisdom, the soil that brought life to our gardens, the birds that sang us their calming melodies, the sun that brought us strength, the rain that has quenched us, the bees that pollinated our fruits and the wind that has kissed our skin. Calling this special place home is a blessing.

Thank you to my mother, who has always supported me in my wild escapades. This book and this special place we've cultivated are a tribute to her. May her cup overflow a million times over for the abundance she has given in this life.

A very special thank-you to my soul family that has lifted me up throughout my life. The experiences we've shared and the lessons you have taught me have greatly shaped who I am, this body of work and my goal in this life. Thank you Kamryn, Emma Kosyla, Kiko Spears, Johanan Bohorquez, Adriana Reloba, Lea Marie Logan, George Dellinger, Daphne Jeanette Jordan, Latha Jay and many more.

A massive thank-you to my editor, Madeline Greenhalgh, and Page Street Publishing for seeing the potential of what I wanted to share and believing in my work. Together, we crafted a beautiful piece of work that I am proud to share with the world.

About the Author

Brian Brigantti is a gardener and content creator based in Morrison, Tennessee. There, he spends his time growing abundance for his family and sharing his ventures with a dedicated audience of over two million on social media. Brian discovered gardening in the wake of the pandemic as a means to grow his own food and reconnect with the land. Having absolutely no experience gardening from an upbringing in the city of Chicago, Brian still has much to learn, but his love for the Earth and its creatures radiates through everything he does. A few short years later, with his blossoming passion for gardening, he now pursues gardening full-time with the hopes of inspiring a shift back to the Earth where we can all cultivate the world's limitless abundance in harmony.

Index

T

Tagore, Rabindranath, 127
three-bin composting, 72
Three Sisters technique, 90
thyme, 125
tilling, 55–56, 78
time
    for gardening, 38, 132–133
    to start garden, 52–53
tomatoes, 87, 88, 117, 136
tools, 57
topsoil, 79
toxic chemicals. See chemicals
transplantation, of seedlings, 53, 101, 102
trees, 84, 127–130
true self, 16

V

vertical plantings, 39, 46

W

water, 38, 43, 79
watering, 26
    container gardens, 64–65
    by hand, 19
    needs, 38, 84, 86, 133–134
    raised beds, 64
water vapor, 130
weather conditions, 86
weed barriers
    laying down, 58–59
    for raised beds, 64
    soaking, 59

weeding, 135
weeds, 62, 64, 135
wildlife, 37, 39, 84, 129, 144
winter, 143, 144, 147
winter squash, 120
wood chips, 60, 73
wood frames, for raised beds, 62
World War II, 78
worms, 56, 59

Z

zucchini, 120